Dear Sally

MARGARET PEAT

Dear Sally

First Published August 2010 by Life Publications, Merthyr Tydfil, South Wales, UK.

Cover design by Graham Alder
ISBN 978-0-9561996-8-3

E–mail: KMPeat@aol.com

Life Publications

Dedication

To Sally

And all my other friends

Who've helped me cry
Until I've laughed

And made me laugh
Until I've cried

You are so special!

Commendations

The collection of letters that reveal Margaret's fascinating journey over 20 years will encourage and inspire you to live your dream. The details of her every day life, woven together with the preparation and guidance of the Holy Spirit is like admiring a rich tapestry of a woman totally devoted to God.

Marilyn Glass

Marilyn is the wife of the General Superintendent of the Elim Churches in the UK and inspirational leader of "Aspire", a rapidly expanding ministry for women in the UK and overseas.

Some people have the uncanny knack of sneaking up on you when you least expect it – finding that sweet spot inside where all pretences and protests just melt. Margaret is such a story teller. Her honesty welcomes the reader to be a sojourner – to grasp the hand of God and walk. Such a gift is rare. This book is about that amazing adventure, her amazing adventure. Thank you Margaret for sharing it. I highly recommend this book.

Simon Foster

Simon ministered alongside Kevin and Margaret for three years and became the succeeding minister of Glasgow Elim Church. He is currently Senior Pastor of Elim Bristol and is a member of the National Leadership Team of Elim, UK.

Who would have thought that letters written 20 years ago would one day become a book that so clearly demonstrates the Father Heart of God? At the time, Margaret's letters encouraged me to pursue my own destiny and live the dream. Since then I have observed Margaret as she has grown and developed into a powerful woman of God. I pray that by reading *Dear Sally,* you will journey towards discovering how much God loves you and His perfect plan for your life.

Sally

Sally has known Margaret for nearly 40 years. She has three grown up children and currently heads up a primary school in the Midlands. Alongside her husband she is also very involved in local church leadership.

Contents

Introduction

Something about this book caught your eye! What was it? Was it the cover? Was it the title? Or do you have a dream to start to live, or a future to find?

That's what life is all about. Life is about moving forward. Finding our future. Living our dream.

In my first two books, *The White Elephant* and *The Seagull* I share many real life stories of how God came and met individuals exactly where they were, how He brought hope to the hopeless, and enabled many earthbound sparrows to soar into the heavenlies on wings like eagles.

Dear Sally is my story. In your hand you have my story, as I left Derby, and became a minister's wife in Glasgow, and intertwined throughout, if you've read the other books, there may be people you recognise or places you feel you've been.

Everyone has a story, and a story or a testimony can be a powerful thing. In court it is a testimony which often seals the case. At the doctors, our story determines their actions. In marketing, the claim of the salesman does not convince us, but the personal experience of the buyer of the product does. A testimony for a Christian is a personal description of our experience and God's involvement in that. People can then identify with that experience. That is the key to a testimony's power. Someone's testimony enables us to use their past to launch into our future. I hope that you can use my past to launch into your future!

Sally is a good friend. She and I attended the local church together and met and married our husbands, who also, were close friends. All of us are still very involved in church and very committed to our Father God. In 1982, we moved with our husbands from the church where we had found God and which had carefully nurtured our lives for several years, to the City Centre Elim Church in Derby. We then continued our journey in that place. By 1990, Sally and her husband had three lovely children and in July of the same year, we felt the call of God to move from Derby, to take on our own church in Glasgow, Scotland.

Remember the days when you used to write letters, before e-mails, faxes, texts, Facebook and Twitter? A few months ago, Sally presented me with a set of letters which I sent to her during my first few years in Glasgow. Back then, letters were my lifeline and in your hand you hold part of my life.

This book is based on those letters, and they are proof that sometimes it's not easy to start to live a dream.

It is 20 years since those days. God has led us and is continuing to lead us into His plans for our lives. We, like you, are moving forward. Kevin and I have the privilege of ministering for our Father God in many different places in the UK, and also in various parts in the world. But without these vital steps which I eventually learned, the path would have been harder and the way darker. I am still learning.

Something about this book caught your eye! What was it? Was it that you want to pay the price to live your dream? I do hope so.

It is my prayer that you find yourself closer to that dream, through and because of "Dear Sally…"

1

In 1990

* *Margaret Thatcher was replaced by John Major as Prime Minister*
* *The Three Tenors became major world stars*
* *"Home Alone" and "Pretty Woman" were hit films*
* *Cliff Richard became the first person in history to have a number one chart success in five consecutive decades with his Christmas number one*
* *Nelson Mandela was released from prison in South Africa*

August 4th, 1990

Dear Sally,

I really am here! We left at midday, last Tuesday Kevin's mum waving wildly at the front gate, trying to be brave!

It took us two hours for the men to load up the furniture van and once I'd cleaned round, I left a bottle of something for the couple who are going to rent our house and then we loaded up Michael the dog, Cocky the cockatiel and Golly the goldfish into the car and left Jasmine Close, Derby, for good.

Unfortunately, by the time we got to Nottingham Road, the dog had a fight with the bird and we had to unload everybody and rearrange ourselves, sitting next to someone we could travel in harmony with for the rest of the journey! A delighted Michael the dog was in the front with Kevin, and I travelled up to Scotland with the goldfish bowl between my knees and the bird cage under my arm!

The weather was very hot but it was exciting all the same to be setting off on the rest of our life. When we crossed the Scottish border, Kev put on the radio and it happened to be playing bagpipes! Wonderful timing for our arrival in Scotland. I'd never been to Scotland before, except for the church interview back in May. God moves in mysterious ways!

We arrived at Joseph and Mae's home in the Gorbals, mid afternoon. They did the same as us some thirty years ago, moving to Glasgow, but they came from abroad. Within a few minutes, felt I'd known them for years. They are wonderful people.

It was later that evening once we were tucked up in their spare bedroom that I felt a bit homesick. "How can you feel homesick?" I asked myself. "You've only been here three hours!" I told Kev. "Pretend you're on holiday," he said and then turned over and went to sleep!

I lay listening to the never ending traffic on the street below. I was in the Gorbals, the razor gang capital of the 1930s. I remembered the article I'd read a month before stating that through the 80s it has been the most dangerous place in the UK. July 1990 now... I hoped the doors were locked!

I awoke early the next morning. I immediately wondered where I was, and then I remembered! It wasn't a dream. It was real. Couldn't believe I'd left the city I'd lived in for 33 years. I wasn't sure I liked the feeling which was increasing by the minute.

Last Wednesday was a blazingly hot day in Glasgow. By the time midday arrived, the furniture was arranged in our newly painted apartment. As I stood at the door and watched the huge van drive slowly away, heading back to Derby, I wasn't sure if I wanted to go too. I stood and watched the van disappear round the corner and then walked back into the house.

In the kitchen, we found the cupboards had been filled with food ready for our arrival. What a kind thing to do. Later that afternoon, Jack, one of our church deacons called to see how we were getting on. We met Jack at the interview and had spoken several times to him on the phone since. It was really good to see someone we felt we knew, even just a little bit.

There was so much to do on that first day, curtains to hang and boxes to unpack and I set to work making our house into a home. A little while later, I wandered to the back window and watched as our upstairs neighbours held a barbeque with their friends on the back lawn. "How strange," I thought, "for us to be in a city of three quarters of a million people and know nobody!" It was a very strange feeling having no friends round the corner and no family nearby.

The next day was Thursday and we needed the car tax renewing. There is a Post Office across the road from our house so I went there first. The guy said we needed to go to a different Post Office, but he had a really broad Glaswegian accent and I couldn't understand where he was telling me to go (although I had my suspicions!) In the end, I had to get a paper and pen out of my bag and ask him to write it down! I bought a street map and found my way to the Post Office in Castlemilk. It looked like Fort Apache, the Bronx. It had bars at the windows and there was more barbed wire than bricks. Not at all like Chaddesden Post Office on Woods Road! Anyway, by that time I was so relieved to be able to get the tax on the car that I braved the building and bought the tax and then found the way home.

The induction service went well. It was our Wedding Anniversary on the same day. We both remembered it this year! Our first miracle up here! The place was packed out and people came from all the other churches around. It was a good, if not very nerve wracking-evening. The next morning, we met our church for the first time. About fifty people for the first morning and the weekend seemed to go OK. Dave Simpson from Derby Church came up for the induction which was great, until he went home and then I felt very homesick.

Well that's the first few days done. Derby seems so far away right now but God is with us. I'm really glad He is.

With love and best wishes,
Margaret

PS Spoke to an elderly lady on Sunday evening. She asked if I'd been coming long to the church. I said I was the new Pastor's wife. She said she thought I was one of the teenagers in the church – what a nice woman!

PPS I think her name is Mrs Christie.

August 20th, 1990
(2 weeks later…)

Dear Sally,

Hope you and everyone in your house are well. Thanks for the letter. We are settling in nicely and the time has gone quite quickly, though in other ways we seem to have been gone from Derby for ages and ages.

I have just cleaned up from tea and settled down by the fire. Michael the dog is lying in his brand new dark-green-with-paws-on basket in the corner, looking ultra pleased with himself. He's already begun storing up half chewed biscuits and anything else he finds in the food line. I suppose it's for if he gets hungry in the night! He's been such a good dog except that he keeps thinking we've got burglars upstairs and barking in time with the bumps. He's not used to apartment living!

Glasgow is the city of culture for this year, and it looks great. Not at all as I'd imagined Glasgow to be. It's really smart in the city centre but this afternoon, when I was down there, the buildings seemed so tall, the roads so wide and the pavements so busy. I think I'm having withdrawal symptoms for St Peter's Street and Sadler Gate! I was sitting next to someone on the bus, who by the time she got off, had told me more about herself than any of my closest friends who I've known for years. Latest operations, next door neighbour's marriage situation, problems with her daughter etc, etc. I felt like I'd known her all my life. Needs getting used to, these close encounters of the Glasgow kind!

It's really strange because everyone is new and I'm continually thinking what to talk about. I have a list of subjects in my head for gaps in the conversation. I would just love to pop to Lynne's on a Monday night like I've done for the past five years or do something familiar. It's all so different. Will improve soon.

Our little flat is becoming a home now. It's called a four in a block with four rooms plus a kitchen and bathroom. It's a downstairs flat so the front door is at the side and it opens into a hall. At the end of the hall is the sitting room on the right, our bedroom is straight ahead and the spare room is on the left. The other tiny spare room and the kitchen are off the sitting room. It's been interesting, fitting in all the stuff from our house. There's things everywhere.

Throughout the week Kevin is down at the church between nine and ten thirty daily and then out visiting for the rest of the day. Different people come in to see him for counselling or just to catch up. It's amazing, talking to all the people. Hearing twenty or thirty different versions of events in the church does give you a very good overall picture of the place.

I have been joining Kev on a lot of the visits. The tenements are something new. They are rows of high buildings four floors up joined together all down the street so there's not much sun around where they are standing. Never been in one before. Now I seem to have been in hundreds over the last couple of weeks! You enter through a door which opens into a “close” (that is a hall and stairway leading to the four floors). All floors have three doors, each leading into a flat, so the tenements are known as 0/1 or 3/2 or whatever, depending on which floor it's on and what number flat.

God has been so good and the church meetings have been really blessed. But the honeymoon period is still here! The people are very friendly though it's hard to catch what's being said when they talk in a group. They are very easy to talk to because you generally can’t get a word in anyway. When I'm counselling and someone is upset, it's hard to decipher what they are saying. Sometimes I just have to take a hopeful guess!

Everybody has a meal or a snack for you when you visit and usually slips a jar of jam, piece of cake or a packet of biscuits into our hands when we leave. I think we're going to stop arranging the visits in advance as due to the wonderful hospitality up here we're going to be enormous by Christmas! One day, we ate three very tasty meals by the time we got home. I felt a bit like the Vicar of Dibley. We've decided to go unannounced in future.

Well I think that's all your questions. I am a bad letter writer but I am doing really well so far. It's amazing how missing people makes you put pen to paper. Would appreciate your prayers Thursdays and Sundays. It's quite nerve-wracking on the meeting days.

See you soon,
Love Margaret

August 31st, 1990
(about two weeks later…)

Dear Sally,

Thanks for your letter. Glad to hear you are busy.

No doubt it takes a lot of the day going backwards and forwards to school with the kids. It's a great place to get to know people isn't it? Same place, same time every day. I know when I was teaching in Derby I got to know some mums very well.

Can't believe the weather here! It was glorious sunshine for our first five days. It rained on the Sunday and it's been raining ever since. It seems to have been raining for the whole of August and the rain goes horizontal here too as well as down!

The schools began after the long holiday in the middle of

Dear Sally

August. Really strange. Feels like the middle of the summer holidays to me. Saw all the uniform clad kids setting off on the Thursday morning on their way to their new classes.

I was reading a little about the history of the church yesterday – revival meetings by George Jeffreys the evangelist who began many of the Elim Churches in Scotland. Ten thousand people at the final meeting of the month, queues of people waiting to get in and hundreds turned away. Healings and creative miracles and 1,400 converted during the month. I know that for a long time, the church was 500 plus. It's our passion to see those days again.

On another note, slight mishap last week! I drove into a post in the middle of the road and caused nearly £700 of damage to the car. Well, it was pouring with rain and I was turning right into a side road and how did I know that there was a post with a keep left arrow in the middle of the road? I was very popular! We were stuck because we couldn't drive the car but very kindly, the church hired one for us for a week. It's going to be mended this week. What was amazing was that by the time I arrived at the evening prayer night, the whole church knew about it and wanted to know every detail. Feels a bit like living on a stage. Will need to get used to that. Anyway keep that to yourself as I told Kevin's mum we had a little scrape. Don't want her worrying.

Well I will sign off now. Have got a thought about when we come down to the wedding but will mention it next time I write. Too late now. Sorry about the change of pen. Had a break.

Write soon,
Love Margaret

*

Events don't cause
our feelings

It is our interpretation
of events which cause our feelings

*

God's Thoughts

> *"At the time, discipline isn't much fun. It always feels like it's going against the grain. Later of course, it pays off handsomely, for it's the well-trained who find themselves mature in their relationship with God. So don't sit around on your hands! No more dragging your feet! Clear the path for long-distance runners..."*
>
> Hebrews 12:11-13a

> *"We can be so sure that every detail in our lives of love for God is worked into something good."*
>
> Romans 8:28

Your Thoughts

There were so many ways that I could have interpreted events differently during those first few months. Our interpretation of events and how we react to them after they have taken place really does make a difference to how we feel, both long term and short term. I was interpreting the events in my life in a way that made me feel isolated and insecure instead of a way that made me feel expectant and excited.

Ask God to show you an event in the last week, month or year, which was pretty tough to go through and complete the space below with your thoughts...

What?

When?

Who?

Where?

You cannot change this event but you can change your interpretation of the event. Now ask Him to show you how you can interpret this differently. Difficult events often strengthen us in many different ways. Maybe that is a thought you can develop.

Prayer

Acknowledge before Him that events don't cause your feelings, but that it's your interpretation of events which cause those feelings.

Ask God to get involved in your reactions to negative events in your life.

Repent for the times you have made incorrect interpretations and make a choice to look for God's perspective in every situation you come up against.

Bible Meditation

Now get comfortable, find a quiet place, and select one of the Bible verses in this chapter. Read it again and take as long as you have to allow God the Father to imprint it deeply on your heart. Focus on a word or two. Apply the whole verse to your day, to your week or to your life. Be still in His presence. Allow the words, sharper than a two edged sword, to touch your heart. Be prepared to hear His still small voice whisper to you. Be prepared to be amazed, challenged, enriched. Be prepared for God to touch your life.

2

September 4th, 1990
(a few days later…)

Dear Sally,

Thanks for the letter and also the run down on current phone charges! Please forgive my mistakes but it's late at night. Kevin is watching a video so I thought I'd drop you a line. I always open the mail. Kevin rarely reads it but if there's one from you or his mum, he's always opened it already. I think he likes the news! I like letters because you can read them again. Phone calls only happen once. As I said before, people are very friendly here but it's different, not having friends round the corner. Have been feeling a bit lonely today but I'm sure we'll be getting to know people better as time goes on.

We are enjoying the new challenge in ministry. God has really blessed the church throughout August. We thought we would have a quiet start and gently ease ourselves in but it has not been quite like that, though as I mentioned before, we're probably still in the honeymoon period. People say the honeymoon lasts between three days and three months so we are waiting for the bang!

We have a great worship band so I don't play keyboard or piano here. I do miss being involved in the worship. No doubt there will be different things open up for me within the church in time. I have made myself chief litter-picker-upper for the time being!

Last Sunday we had a healing meeting and Kevin told the people at the end to come back next week and hear the testimonies of healing. We are praying now that some will have been healed.

My dad died one year ago on September 11th. As we were coming down for the wedding on Thursday night anyway, I'm thinking of popping down slightly earlier in the week then I can visit the crematorium on the 11th. I've not decided definitely yet but I'd quite like to go the first year. Maybe we can get together then at some point?

Have been to see a social worker this week to find out about drugs. Not for us (yet). Drugs and drink seem to be a big problem in this city, as in many others. Apparently, you can get drugs from the ice cream man! The other night, we were driving through Castlemilk around 11pm and passed an ice-cream van. It had stopped at the side of the road and there was a queue of people, mostly men, waiting for ice-cream! I didn't really think anything of it but it was Kevin that commented on the popularity of 99s and double scoops at 11 o'clock on a Monday night! We've since found out that something else is pretty popular too. I think you need a password or something. We've not found the right passwords yet! That particular road is quite a place. Steve, who lives around there, said you get to know your neighbours very quickly in his area because you're forever at the window, watching the fights in the street!

What I found even more astonishing than the ice-cream van thing, was that the other night, there was an article in the

Evening Times about a pensioner round the corner from the church getting arrested for having a sideline, drug dealing by selling his prescription drugs to the teenagers! "Mick the Fix" was his name. Where have all the sweet OAPs gone?

Anyway on that note, must sign off and dry my hair now. Short letter this time. Thanks again for writing. Love to Ron and the children.

Write soon.

With lots of love,
Margaret

September 18th, 1990

(two weeks later…)

Dear Sally,

Thanks for your letter. Hope everyone is well. I would imagine you're quite ready for the kids to go back to school – will be thinking about Jake as he starts this time doesn't he? Hope Brittany is feeling a bit better now.

Thanks for the phone call the other night. It was good to hear a familiar accent. Getting used to the Glaswegian a little more. Last week Kevin came down from the platform to sit on the front row as he couldn't tell whether the worship leader was speaking Glaswegian or speaking in tongues! Still working on it!

It was great to be in Derby for a few days, especially for my birthday. Lynne cooked me my favourite meal of chicken and cashew nuts. Lovely to see everyone at the wedding though it was so hard to leave at the end of it. We got back about 2am. The next morning, it seemed like everyone had been to a wedding the night before because there were only forty two folk at the meeting and it was really hard going. Still the evening was better. The night numbers are increasing well and there's a real buzz at those meetings.

Last Sunday, we had a baptism. The church had worked hard inviting people and there were 133 people there, about 60 more than usual, (there's usually somewhere in the 70s in the evening). We were very pleased when two more people made decisions. It was a great evening and by the end of the night, Kev was smiling, I was smiling and even the dog was smiling!

Kev took his first leadership meeting on Tuesday night with Jack, who I've mentioned to you before and also Joseph, who we stayed with for our first night in Glasgow. There are two more leaders, one in his twenties, a nice guy and Wally, who is a pensioner and who told Kevin that I was the reason he'd voted for him to get the job! Very nice man!

We went to visit a newcomer to the church who lives at Blackhill. It was quite scary getting out of the car as most of the tenements had been boarded up and it was a really rough area. Tom was telling us about the Ice Cream wars in the 1980s. He's lived round there for years. The ice cream vans stocked ice cream but also liquor and cigarettes and drugs. They were also a good way of laundering dirty money and selling on stolen goods. There was a constant battle for "turf" and "territory" and various methods were used to persuade the ice cream salesmen to give up their patch. They were getting attacked, bricks through the windows, beatings, nails in the tyres, sugar in petrol tanks and basically bullied out of business. One had his house set on fire. He had been attacked at least twice in his ice cream van but the fire in the house resulted in their family of six dying in the fire. No one in the area would give information. It was considered too dangerous to speak to the police.

Apparently “Ponderosa” is quite near where Tom lives. Ponderosa is the home of the Glasgow Godfather but that’s for another letter.

We've discovered a couple of avid Abba fans in the flat above us. They hold Abba parties until four in the morning! The problem is that it's usually on a Saturday night. At around 4am, Sunday morning last weekend, we were sitting in bed having a cup of tea. The music was so loud it was as if they were in the same room. I hope the people next to us don't think it's us! A great start to the Sunday services! I was so tired during the service the next day. Don’t mind Abba music but not till four in the morning.

We hope to go away in October to Arran. Arran is an island off the west coast of Scotland. We took a drive to Ardrossan the other day to check where we board the ferry (not being accustomed to going on islands, being from the Midlands). We were just driving down the road when suddenly, blue flashing lights behind us. The police told us they never give warnings in Scotland and booked us on the spot for exceeding the speed limit. A costly trip! Anyway, when we got to the ferry terminal, we peered over the wall and we could see the peaks of the mountains rising into the clouds. It looked like something from Enid Blyton’s *Secret Island* book. We're going Monday to Saturday but it's not finalised yet. Can’t wait! Never been to a real island before!

On a Monday we usually go out for the day. It’s a good break and then Tuesday, we are ready to start the week again. At the moment, it’s totally consuming in thought, time and energy.

Just about time for bed now. Kevin and the dog are arranged in different chairs in front of the TV. There was a brief dispute between them a few minutes ago, about the occupancy of the chair by the fire. Kevin won. Anyway I won’t keep you any

longer. Give our love to everyone your end.
Write soon.

Lots of love,
Margaret

PS It's still raining! Jimme came up to me at church last Sunday and said not to worry, it doesn't rain all the time. He said, “Come December it stops raining... it starts snowing!”

October 14th, 1990
(a month later…)

Dear Sally,

Hope you are well.

Today is Sunday. It is 11.20pm and my favourite part of the day. Hope your day went well.

Today we have had two very good meetings. Twelve people came into membership this morning and Kev spoke on having a faith that allows God to do what He wants. Ten folk came forward for prayer at the end and there was a powerful presence of God. A couple of weeks ago, we had a healing meeting and one woman testified this morning that she had been to the hospital this week and the stomach ulcer which she had had for several years had disappeared. A lad also testified that his great aunt had suffered a stroke recently and he had stood on behalf of her. He said she is a lot better and she has started to use her arm which has been paralysed since 1957. Tonight Kev spoke on a Christian’s commitment. There were 91 of us there which is good for us, and as there has been over 90 people there for four weeks now, we were really pleased. It was a good day.

We went up to Mrs Christie's for tea last week. She is such a lovely lady, so positive and always looking on the bright side. She lives a little way out of Glasgow on the south side of the city. Her road is all tree lined with spaced out houses and a big park at the end of the road. We stayed about two hours and it made me think a lot afterwards. She's in her eighties, doesn't walk well and she can't get out easily but her outlook on life is amazing. An inspiration. Also felt a little bit like home too, so it was a good day.

We had Ann Taylor up a few weeks ago for a few days. We took her round the city one evening, round Anderston Bus Station which is the area where the prostitutes hang out. It's a grid of streets on a steep hill and each girl has their own street corner with a guy watching a few girls each. Apparently the higher up the street you stand, the more you can charge. That's what Anna told us anyway who used to be on the streets.

We went to Cathkin Braes after that, which is a hillside above Glasgow where you can see the whole of the city and beyond. It's an amazing sight of thousands of lights if you go at night so it was about 11.30pm when we ended up there. We were standing in the middle of the field looking out at the Glasgow lights shining up from the city below when we heard two vans pull off the road and onto the edge of the field. We stood really still and they got out and started transferring stuff from one van to the other. After it had all been done, they got back into their vehicles and left. We were still standing in the middle of the field! I think Ann was a bit freaked by it and I can't say I was comfortable either. We thought she'd seen enough for one night. We had a good weekend but after spending the whole weekend reassuring her she was OK, on her last night, there was an armed robbery at the Post Office across the road. Not sure if she'll come back… It certainly was an interesting visit!

Dear Sally

How are things in Derby? Is Jake still enjoying school? And Chloe?

I've been called for Jury duty the week that we planned to go to Arran. I rang the office and they said to wait and see if I get selected to sit on the jury and then explain about my holiday. Let's just hope it turns out OK. Praying too.

Michael has settled in well (for a dog!). He loves his walks on the different parks we've been to. There's some really big ones here and he loves to run free off lead. Funny how dogs know how you feel isn't it? Whenever I've had a little weep, he's got up from the other room and come to find me. He looks up at me with those beautiful brown eyes as though to say, "It's all going to be OK you know." Anyone with a dog would understand. I love being around the house with him all day – he's a great dog and very precious just now.

Well I will sign off now as we are going to bed. Hope your creche ministry is going well. No doubt you've reorganised the whole thing by now. Will let you know whether I get to Arran or not and if so whether our adventures match up to Enid Blyton's in *The Secret Island*! Or whether I get to do Jury duty instead!

Write soon,

Love and best wishes,
Margaret xx

*

You can't change your feelings
but you can change your thoughts,
and your thoughts will change
your feelings

*

God's Thoughts

> *"Summing it all up, friends, I'd say you'll do best by filling your minds and meditating on things true, noble, reputable, authentic, compelling, gracious – the best, not the worst; the beautiful, not the ugly; things to praise, not things to curse."*
>
> Philippians 4:8

> *"We use our powerful God-tools for smashing warped philosophies, tearing down barriers erected against the truth of God, fitting every loose thought and emotion and impulse into the structure of life shaped by Christ."*
>
> 2 Corinthians 10:5

Your Thoughts

Some of my feelings were negative I must admit. If I had only realised earlier that although I couldn't change my feelings, I could have changed my thoughts and the rest would have followed.

Use the space below (and the blank pages at the end too if you need) to record all your negative thoughts for one day. Then read through these thoughts and make a change to each one of them. Your new thought needs to be believable, not necessarily just the opposite of your old thought.

eg: Thought: That bus driver was so rude. How dare he treat me like that. I feel so angry.

Change: That bus driver was so rude. He's obviously had a really bad day or got big problems. Never mind… nothing personal.

THOUGHT	*CHANGE*

Prayer

Make a choice before God to walk in mercy rather than stand in judgement as you live each day.

Ask Him to make you aware of the negative thoughts which pervade your day.

Pray that He will help you to change these thoughts as they happen and that the new thoughts will change your feelings and your new feelings will enhance your life.

Bible Meditation

Now get comfortable, find a quiet place, and spend time meditating on the Bible verses earlier in this chapter.

Note: More of Jimme's story can be found in "The White Elephant." More of Mrs Christie's story can be found in "The Seagull."

3

October 31st, 1990
(two weeks later…)

Dear Sally,

Thanks for your letter. Hope you and the family are well.

We're just back from the Isle of Arran. We went on Monday and came back on Saturday. We had a great holiday. We walked miles and Michael fell off some stepping stones into the river and the next day got stuck in a bog up to his neck! By the time we got back to where we were staying, the mud had solidified and dried in the sun and he was a cause of great amusement to everyone who saw him. He looked mildly like he was having a nervous breakdown for the rest of the day! Great to take a break though. It really gave me a chance to take stock a bit. Decided to be more positive about the more stretching aspects of life just now.

I think I mentioned that I was called for Jury duty last week. I went on the first day to the Court. It's a bit different here in Scotland. There's a Procurator Fiscal instead of a Judge. I turned up where I should be and waited to see if I would be picked. If so, they had instructed me to take my holiday details in to see if I could take my holiday instead. They called the names and I wasn't one of them. I found out then that it was the case of the armed robbery at the Post Office across the road from us, where I go every other day, so I don't know if I could have been on the Jury or not after all. Not quite sure how it works.

We were delighted with the weather on the holiday. We had two dull days and three sunny days. I had forgotten what the sun looked like. The sun shone and I had nothing to wear. It has rained none stop since we got back!

Our car was broken into just before we went away. They took the cassette radio but nothing else. Someone said we could buy it back at the Barra’s! The Barra's is a huge market where you can buy anything and everything and the place where apparently, if you get something stolen on Tuesday night, you can buy it back on Wednesday. That’s what they told us anyway. I think we'll just get another radio instead! It's amazing we didn't hear anything as the car is right on the street outside our bedroom window.

Passed “Ponderosa” this week on the way to visit someone. Ponderosa is the home of Arthur Thompson who is known by the press as the “Glasgow Godfather”. Ponderosa was a row of smaller houses and he bought the far left and far right and I think the others in between moved out. Tom was telling us that not long ago there was a breakfast swoop by the police on the house with helicopter, guns, dogs and shields. The street was sealed off and there were crowbars and sledgehammers used too. Could certainly be an experience living across the road.

Living in a big city is really different. The road outside is quite busy and the street never seems quiet. There are taxis sounding their horns and revving most of the night and people walking past talking loudly till the early hours of the morning. It's like sleeping on the pavement being downstairs. It’s sometimes a bit scary when there are people right outside the window. It sounds like they're about to climb through.

Have you any news about your house yet? I forgot to ask you. Is the house you want still for sale? The people above us had a party on Saturday night until 3.30am. Abba again. I had *Voulez Vous* going round my head all the way through the morning service!

Thanks for the invite to the meal – tell Rita that it was the thought that counts. Glad you had a good time. Really miss everyone in Derby. You don't value long term relationships until they're not there. Really strange going into church and not knowing people. It's easy to feel shy and not talk to people but I've taken to throwing myself into conversations, as though I'd known them for years. It works much better!

Sunday was OK. It rained all day. Hamden Park is just up the road from the church and the football played extra time till just before the service so we had only 78 people in the evening. Hope it goes up a bit next week. We prayed for a lady with a swollen knee and by the end of the meeting it had gone down to nearly normal. That was amazing!

How is crèche going? Are you still in charge? Jim said you would like to help with youth club in some way – we said very good idea! You'll soon be running the church at this rate!

Well better go now.

Write soon,
Love from Margaret xxx

November 6th, 1990
(a week later…)

Dear Sally,

Thanks for your letter. Hope you are all well.

We have let our house in Derby again from November 5th. Bonfire night. I think they move in next Monday. It is supposed to be for six months, but then the last tenants were, and they stayed only six weeks! I think for the amount of rent they pay, people realize they can borrow money and buy their own house or something. Anyway we'll see.

I started to write this letter at 10am this morning and what with one thing and another, I've finally picked it up again at 7.40pm. Someone from church called for two minutes and stayed two hours! Quite nice really.

How is the outreach going? Still it's hard to tell after one week isn't it? Hope the additional members of your family don't stay too long (the nits I mean). It's an infant teacher's hazard! Now the nit nurse doesn't come, they go round and round the class.

There's a women's hostel across the road from the church which houses seventy six homeless women. There's forever police cars arriving outside and often fire engines (for some reason). There's also usually a man or two hanging around outside, waiting I guess for someone in there. A lot of the older ones are alcoholics who have lost their home and a lot of the younger ones are prostitutes who you see getting picked up in the evening, being taken to their patch to begin their night's work. One of them brought some of her clothes across to the church in the week to see if Kevin wanted to buy something for me. That would certainly have brightened up the morning meeting! A few of the women come across to the church. I went over to say hello to Bridget the other day. I wasn't allowed in the resident's room but I could sit in the common room with her. Interesting collection of women! There were four ladies sitting where we were while I was there. One that smiled a lot, two that talked a lot and one that hugged anything that moved!

We had a bonfire party at church on Monday night. I only went to the last half as I had an interview for a teaching job. It's a private job for a Jewish family in Giffnock. They asked all about my church so I doubt I've got much chance of getting the position. I've heard nothing yet. How's your job going? The hours are quite convenient aren't they? I'm going to write to a few schools about a bit of supply work soon. It's not quite so urgent now that our house is rented again, but I must do something soon or I'll get used to being a lady of leisure!

Well I'll sign off now. *Coronation Street* has finished and I'm going to dry the dishes. I went to see the Burrell Collection at Pollok Park this afternoon with Jan from church. I was quite looking forward to getting to know her better and I really enjoyed it. I've been shattered ever since the walk round the park. It's 365 acres. We didn't walk quite that far, but nearly.

Hope you had a good birthday. It was the only card I could find at 11.15pm. Still it's the thought that counts.

Have enclosed a church programme. Not sure what happened to it this month. I don't think the photocopier was feeling well (or the photocopy-ist). Still I've put it in anyway.

Another person who wasn't feeling well was David Simpson. Following his visit for our induction he decided to re-visit. He came up ten days ago and caught flu. He was flat on his back for five days in our spare room and then needed a few more days to feel well enough to drive himself the three hundred miles back to Derby. Came up, got flu, got well, went home! What a trip. They're never going to believe him at work.

Write soon,
Love Margaret

November 21st, 1990
(Two weeks later…)

Dear Sally,
Thanks for your letter which I received today. Glad to hear all is fine down your end. Interesting happenings!

It seems I have started lessons on Robbie Burns! The week before last, I picked up Mrs McNaught, one of the old ladies in the church. She loves Robbie Burns and every week I get treated to a rendition of his poetry. It was the bit about "to see ourselves as others see us" or something, this week. Anyway, if I pick her up much longer, I'll know the entire poem start to finish!

Today, I've been teaching at a school about three miles from here. Many of the Glasgow schools are huge Victorian two storey buildings, quite austere from the outside. It's the first time I've actually been inside one. It's quite strange not knowing where anything is and learning names all over again. For saying I've taught for thirteen years in Derby, I was really nervous. I'm back there tomorrow and then again on Monday. I managed to survive till interval today and then mid morning, I happened to look over the balcony (the classrooms are upstairs around a balcony with the hall in the centre down below). The whole school was in the hall apart from my class. They had forgotten to tell me about Assembly. Have you every tried to get 30 kids into a room incognito? It's really difficult deciphering the kids' accents from the other side of the classroom. I'm getting a little better face to face but from the other side of the room the Glaswegian sounds like Chinese! Also, during the calling of the register, I am surmising that from some of the sniggers, my Glaswegian is not yet up to scratch! Some of the names are pretty hard to sight-read! I mean, how do you say McAtamney? Or McEachern? Still it provided some light entertainment for the commencement of the day. Running the Infant Department at Firs Estate seems a doddle in comparison!

There are some interesting people up here. Just got talking to a man over the last couple of weeks who's recently been released from Barlinnie Prison (or Bar-L as it's called). Found out tonight he's a fire bomber – or hopefully an ex-fire bomber! Seemed a really nice guy. Passed Barlinnie Prison yesterday. It's a huge dark foreboding place. You would think that one look at that place would put you off but Wal was saying that many of the criminals consider that time in "Barlinnie Hotel" as it's also known, adds "street cred" to the crime CV! If you can get a chib (facial knife scar) while you're in there that's apparently double street cred if you're in that line of business.

Went in the shop across the road this week. Asked for bacon, but I think bacon must be ham as they gave me ham. Went back for bacon later. Less complicated. Quite enjoying finding out about the differences though some days.

Church doing well. Stan rang to say that Billy Graham will be coming to Glasgow next June. It would be fantastic if that were to happen. A really great opportunity for the church.

It's very cold up here just now. These storage heaters are really hard to work. You put them on at night and they are supposed to let heat out during the day but I don't think we're doing it properly as by afternoon it's cold. It's wet and damp just now but at least the rain is vertical this week instead of horizontal! That's positive isn't it? I wonder if Derby will feel warm when we come down at Christmas…

The church burglar alarm went off again last night. Kevin usually goes down to investigate as he is the first "key holder" on the list but last night, not having had a lot of excitement for at least three days I thought I'd go down too. Kev says he is often there ages before the police come so he keeps a stick in the cupboard to tour the building with in case anyone's still in there. It was really spooky, especially as last weekend someone came to the Sunday night meeting and opened a back window in the building so they could come back in the night and lift all the microphones and my tape recorder! Not as novel as the guy the other week who was taking money out of the offering bag as it was passed round, instead of putting money in!

Anyway better go now. Again, thanks for your letter. Hope children are all well. Glad nits have gone. And Ron.

See you soon,
Love Margaret xxxx

PS Kev told me that a head teacher rang me yesterday to talk about a temporary job which will lead to a permanent one but I wasn't in. He didn't know who it was or what school it was but she's going to ring me back sometime. Would be great to learn to say one set of surnames instead of a different set each week! I'm hoping she'll ring today or tomorrow. I'll let you know when she does.

*

Your expectation can sometimes determine your experience

*

God's Thoughts

> *"A miserable heart means a miserable life; a cheerful heart fills the day with song."*
>
> Proverbs 15:15

> *"Steep your life in God-reality, God-initiative, God-provisions. Don't worry about missing out. You'll find all your everyday human concerns will be met."*
>
> Matthew 6:33

Your Thoughts

Learning to change my expectation was a challenge, but little by little, I was waking up to the idea that often your expectation can affect your behaviour and your behaviour can affect your experience.

Choose one negative situation in your life at this moment and note it below:

____

____

____

____

____

Every day for 31 days, thank God for being with you in this situation and ask Him to work in it. Now start to expect Him to do it.

1 2 3 4 5 6 7 8 9 10 11 12 13 14 15 16 17

18 19 20 21 22 23 24 25 26 27 28 29 30 31

Prayer

Ask God to forgive you for the times when your expectation has determined your experience.

Make a choice before God to expect good things from Him and allow Him daily to work in your experience in a new way.

Bible Meditation

Now get comfortable, find a quiet place, and spend time meditating on the Bible verses earlier in this chapter.

Note: Read the story of Susan who lived in the hostel in "The White Elephant." Read more about Mrs McNaught in "The Seagull".

4

November 28th, 1990
(one week later…)

Dear Sally,

Many thanks for your letter. I must admit, they're always very interesting to read.

What is the weather like down there? It's like Siberia here! Yesterday, we went for a coffee at Drumpellier Loch which is nearby and it was completely frozen over. The ice was a quarter of an inch thick, and that was midday. It seems that the early morning frost which disappears in Derby after an hour or so, stays all day here, then more comes the next night until after a few days, it looks as though it has snowed without ever having snowed at all.

Michael is refusing to sit on the floor at all and will only sit in chairs. At night he waits until we have gone to sleep and then crawls under the quilt from the bottom. If Kev finds him, he kicks him out but if I wake then I must admit, I do sometimes take pity, bless him.

How are you enjoying your job? I would imagine the time goes very quickly being as I've never seen Sainsbury's short of shoppers.

I've got a job. A head teacher rang me last Friday and asked me if I wanted a part time post nine until twelve daily. The hours are ideal. I finish at 10.30 every Friday. The one drawback is that it's fifteen miles from home. I've decided to do it till July and see how the travelling goes. It's about twenty five minutes from home but I'm not sure what the rush hour traffic will be like in the morning.

I worked a couple of days last week at a local school, 95 per cent were from ethnic backgrounds. Again, calling the register was an experience. Longed for the James Smith and Linda Browns of Derby! This time, I couldn't pronounce most of the names! I was planning to do some more hours there but I'm going to my new school tomorrow for the morning, and next week there's now a couple of things on so I'll wait until the week after. Not sure how it will go travelling there every day – I'll let you know.

Did you get the cards from Kev's mum? I wondered if you could put them in the church post box near Christmas. We usually send lots to church but I've only written those so far. I thought we'll see about any others later.

We called in Castlemilk this week to visit Wally, our OAP deacon. What a lovely man. When we got out of the car we had to walk through a shopping area. There was an off licence, betting office, post office and a few other shops. There were loads of people sitting around on the floor and on steps, drinking cans of lager or whatever. As we walked past them, everyone stopped talking and watched us walk past. I was really glad I wasn't alone. It felt like everybody's eyes were on us until we got inside the house. Wally took one look at us and said, "Dressed like that, they'd think you were the 'polis'!"

Castlemilk is officially the most deprived area in Scotland at the moment. I read that this week. I noticed they are starting to demolish some of the tenements. The boarded up windows and the graffiti all over those waiting for demolition give everywhere a very oppressive atmosphere both for those who live there and those who visit.

Many of the people at church live in tenements. Some of them are small and some are really spacious. Many that survived demolition years ago have very big rooms with huge bay windows and high ceilings. They can fetch very high prices, especially in the West End. I've been to lots of tenements now but what I want to know is… how come everyone seems to live on the top floor? Getting very fit walking up all the stairs. The flats have buzzers and name labels outside on the wall and you can speak to the person from outside before you go in. Apparently, top flats carry a higher risk of being broken into. Middle flats are difficult to escape from whereas thieves can enter and exit via the roof as necessary. Top flats have great views though!

Well we're going to the bank now so I'll finish and post this letter. *Coronation Street* has finished and I don't fancy Val Doonican next so I think venturing out into the minus four degrees would be preferable. The trouble is after ten minutes the dog looks like an icicle. His fur is stiff, standing on end. By the way, since we have been here, he has developed a unique way of welcoming all the people to our house. He wags his tail, rolls on his back and when they bend over him to pat him, he squirts them! Different! Must be something in the air up here?

Well I must go now because Kevin is on his sixth "I'm ready when you are…"

Thanks again for your letter. We miss you.

Lots of love,
Margaret

PS We had ninety nine on Sunday night (but I think it was a fluke). It's usually eighty to ninety so we were really pleased. This week someone has gone to Edinburgh, someone to Jamaica and someone to heaven! So that's three down for a start! See you soon.

December 15th, 1990
(two weeks later…)

Dear Sally,

Thanks for your letter. Glad to hear you are all well and nicely getting into the Christmas spirit! Was everyone in the church at the Crystal Maze game? We've had no end of cards with notes about this maze and saying how good it was. It must have been a brilliant evening.

Well Christmas has come so quickly. Are the children excited? What are they having for Christmas? Today is our Sunday School party which we just popped into for half an hour. The staff had set it up brilliantly. Kev has got pneumonia/bad cold and has gone to bed to recover. The Christmas services start tomorrow so he's keen to get well although enjoying the attention I surmise. Hopefully he'll feel a bit better tomorrow.

In the morning we are having a Senior Citizens' service and Christmas dinner afterwards to which all our OAPs are bringing a friend (well maybe). Mrs Christie is bringing two friends she has coffee with every week. Afterwards we'll have some entertainment and finish off with the usual service in the evening. Trouble is if Kev is sneezing all over the place they'll all have graduated to heaven by January 1st! He has got a chef's outfit and is going to be Manuel from *Fawlty Towers* for the afternoon. It should be a laugh – if he can get out of bed to do it! If he can't, he says I'm leading it! Sincerely hope he's better by then. He can do it much better than I can (and also the outfit doesn't suit me!).

Next week is full of meals, parties etc as no doubt it is for you. Quite a few people from Derby have sent us Christmas cards – it's been lovely to get them. Hope all your services go well. Are you having Carols by Candlelight? With the Protestant and Catholic issues in Glasgow, Carols by Candlelight is not too appropriate in our church!

Do you mind putting more cards in the pigeon holes? Thanks. It's impossible to send to everyone so we've just sent one to the church and one or two to close friends.

How is the job? My official starting date for my January to July job is January 7th. I'm hoping everything goes smoothly. The money will be good. The gift that Derby gave us has been a godsend especially when the house fell through.

It looks very cold down in Derby looking at the forecast. It has not been too bad here this week. Very chilly but mainly blue sky and sunny so as long as you wrap up very well you're OK. I'm sure we're still not working the storage heaters properly.

Well I'd better sign off now. I've got to wrap up two prizes for tomorrow's OAP service and dry my hair. We're supposed to be going to the theatre tonight with someone and his girlfriend if Kev can rise from the dead! We'll see how it goes. We're coming down to Derby after the Christmas Day service up here. Joseph says he will take us round the Barras on Christmas Eve. Looking forward to that.

Hope you can read this. I can't write with this pen very well. Thanks again for your card and letter. Hope the crèche party goes well.

Love and best wishes,
Margaret

PS Do you like the envelope?

In 1991

- * *The Gulf War took place*
- * *Robert Maxwell mysteriously died on his boat in the Canaries*
- * *Paul Gascoigne was a new star in football*
- * *The top film was "Silence of the Lambs"*
- * *Queen's lead singer Freddie Mercury died*

January 4th 1991
(three weeks later…)

Dear Sally,

It was great to see you over Christmas and to get some time to catch up in person. Hope you had a good New Year's Eve.

We had a lovely Christmas with you all. We came up the road on New Year's Eve as you know and arrived in time for the service at church.

That went well and there were a lot of kilts around too. After the bells, we had a party in the back hall with food until about 3am. Nobody seemed to want to go home which was great. When we were travelling back up to Croftfoot it was around

4am and nearly every light was on as we drove through the streets. No wonder both January 1st and 2nd are public holidays in Scotland. It would take that long to get over it. Joseph's wife bought us a steak pie for New Year's Day which is traditional here in Glasgow. It was very nice too!

I didn't get chance to tell you about our Christmas celebrations up here. On Christmas Eve, Joseph took us down to the Barras late on. It was packed out with people and there was an amazing Christmas Eve atmosphere. There were lots of people still buying presents and wrapping paper etc. Joseph says that lots of stuff gets reduced late on and some wait and get their presents then. We had hot dogs and hot chestnuts and with the Christmas songs and the street sellers shouting their wares, it was a great atmosphere. We went to a midnight Christmas Eve service after that and ended with mince pies and steaming hot tea.

On Christmas Day, before driving down to Derby, we took the service at church. The leadership team sang a quintet on the platform and people threw money at them. We had a really good time. Someone gave us a recording of our first Christmas Day service and we were given lots of presents. We went back to Jack and Rita's afterward for Christmas lunch and left mid afternoon for Derby. They are such kind people. By the time we got in the car to drive the six hours to Derby, we felt like we'd already had Christmas – it was great!

Anyway, we are well into the New Year now. Michael's getting used to long distance travel now. Within ten minutes he's usually flat on his back, legs in the air, in the back seat. I remember last Christmas, back in Derby, he unwrapped and ate three large chocolate Santa's and we were running round the park with him hyper at three in the morning. This year anything that remotely smelled, felt or tasted like chocolate was confiscated big time! As he examines all contents of incoming bags to the house and sometimes even helpfully unloads them all onto the floor, I think he is secretly checking just in case another chocolate santa ever crosses his path.

The OAP lunch was a great success. We had a lunch and then sang songs from the olden days. Mrs Christie brought her two friends from a very posh area of Glasgow and some of the ladies from the hostel were there too so it was very interesting. Very moving too, watching everyone singing the carols together and the old songs. Mrs McNaught was also there although I didn't give her a lift. Everyone calls her the Duchess because she always wears furs and pearls. Kev was feeling much better so he led the event, though I was thinking about it for three days beforehand wondering whether I would have to do it!

Anyway, back to reality now, January 4th. Lovely having no new challenges for a whole week in Derby.

I start my new job on Monday. Bit nervous.

Anyway, that's all for now.

Happy New Year,

Much love,
Margaret

*

If you're never stretched, you're no longer growing

*

God's Thoughts

> *"We continue to shout our praise even when we're hemmed in with troubles, because we know how troubles can develop passionate patience in us, and how that patience in turn forges the tempered steel of virtue, keeping us alert for whatever God will do next."*
>
> Romans 5:3-4

> *"I've learned by now to be quite content whatever my circumstances. I'm just as happy with little as with much, with much as with little. I've found the recipe for being happy whether full or hungry, hands full or hands empty. Whatever I have, wherever I am, I can make it through anything in the One who makes me who I am."*
>
> Philippians 4:11-13

Your Thoughts

By this time, I was getting used to being stretched but it still wasn't comfortable. I suppose stretching never is? Challenges in church, school and home situations were part of my life.

Whenever we walk into new territory, it can be a stretching time. We have a choice about some changes such as a promotion, or a house move or a marriage. Some changes we have no choice about such as an unplanned redundancy, a bereavement or a betrayal. Some changes are huge and some changes are smaller, like mine, but they're still stretching. Remember, it may range from being uncomfortable to feeling unbearable but if you're stretched, there is growth taking place and He will be with you in that!

Think back through the last week, month and year in your life. What things were stretching? List them below.

Now ask God to show you in what areas you grew during these difficult times.

____

____

____

____

____

____

Prayer

Thank God for the times you have been stretched and for the growth that has come as a result.

Now examine your heart before God and ask: Have you created a safe haven for yourself? Do you need fresh challenges to jump higher, dive deeper or run further?

Talk to Him about your thoughts.

Bible Meditation

Now get comfortable, find a quiet place, and spend time meditating on the Bible verses earlier in this chapter.

5

January 12th, 1991
(one week later…)

Dear Sally,

We woke last Monday morning to six inches of snow which has been with us all week. Kev gave me a lift to the school where I was due to begin teaching on that day. Was promptly returned home again due to the weather! Shortest first day in history! Thirty seconds. The rest of the week I travelled by train. It's about fifteen minutes in the car to the station and about twenty minutes on the train. I am just getting used to getting up at 7am again after six months! I'd forgotten what 7am looked like but it came back to me in a rush the first morning.

I am blessed with 30, six and seven year-olds from 9am until 12.15pm Monday, Tuesday and Thursday. On Wednesday and Friday I work from 9am until 10.30am. Apparently that works out exactly half time. I hope by summer they will still be a blessing. I've yet to see how the travelling will turn out. Again, as in the last school, it's quite hard understanding the accents from across the room and I'm still trying to get the names right in the register which again include some challenging Scottish surnames! No weekly dinner money, they pay every day, PE every day of the week and no daily assembly, just a once a week hymn practise. All different to Derby.

It is still very cold. I think Michael's growing another coat! He's got twice as much hair at the moment and if you thought he was scruffy before, you should see him now. They say that dogs look like their owners (or is it the other way round?) Either way, I hope not. He greatly resembles the stuffing out of a cushion just now! The weather is bitter and he gets very wet and cold on his walks. Someone told us he should have a coat for his first winter up here but Kev refuses to walk down the road with a dog in a coat! Not good for his image he says! We'll see.

There are lots of foxes around here. I've seen more foxes in the past four months than I've seen in my whole life. They are often in the headlights crossing the road or scurrying through a garden. The other night, we drew up beside a field to walk the dog and there were a couple illuminated in the headlights. We stopped the car and watched them for ages. They were quite amazing to watch rolling about and playing together.

Church wise, Kev took the deacons away last weekend, we're having 7am prayer on Wednesdays at present and nine people were slain in the spirit at the prayer meeting on Thursday night. We're praying for newcomers, the Billy Graham Crusade and for new converts. Things have started moving after Christmas now and we're hoping to pick up a few on numbers over the next month. The weather is so bad that it cuts out most of the older people who catch buses on the very bad days in winter. We're going to our first Burns Supper on 25th January which should be good.

I'm getting to know a few more people. There's a little guy who has been coming to the church since before we came. He's called Wee Eddie. Can't tell a word he's talking about. He turns up for everything! The other week, we had a leaders' meeting and meal together. In walks Wee Eddie, sits down at the table ready for his meal. Nobody seems to bother at all. He talked to us all evening and I couldn't recognize one word except daffodil!

Anyway, better go now.

With love,
Margaret

PS Everyone's got a sticker on the back of their car just now which says "I'm a real Scot from Glasgae." Wouldn't sound quite the same "I'm a real English person from Derby!" Not got quite the same ring…

February 5th, 1991
(three weeks later…)

Dear Sally,

Thanks for your letter. Glad to hear that you are all well. Kev said he enjoyed chatting to you on the phone last week. Glad to hear things are quiet on the home front. When is the AGM? Our AGM is on the 23rd February. Kev will be very glad to get it over with I think. Unpredictable things, AGMs!

School is going well although it's taking me a lot of time in the afternoons marking and preparing work for the next day so I'm almost doing the job full time really. No English kids at all in the whole school so I'm their ethnic minority token!

Took Michael for his annual booster injection and check up this week. It amazes me how pleased he is to see the vet each time he goes. Any dog who is fond of a man who sticks needles into him, shoves a thermometer up his back end and expresses his anal glands every time he meets him has to be an extremely forgiving little dog. I doubt I could stretch to that level of forgiveness!

Church is going well and numbers are still good although we were down to 87 on Sunday night. There were 107 the week before. It does tend to fluctuate a bit. In the morning meeting last week there were 80 which is very good for us. That's gone up from 50 something in August. Altogether on Sunday we had 118 in church through the day so gradually it's going up. Would be good to get everyone there at the same time! I'm still picking Mrs McNaught up on a Sunday morning. I drop Kev off at church then go through to Tory Glen. She never fails to tell me off for being late, even when I'm early! She was telling me last week she was saved at a George Jeffreys' crusade in Glasgow and her passion for George Jeffreys seems to almost match that for Robert Burns. I think the two loves of her life are Robert Burns and George Jeffreys! Her late husband must have had a really hard time competing with those two.

Another person jumped off the Kingston Bridge this week. Kev was talking to someone last week who knows the man who does the dredging in the River Clyde. That means every time someone jumps off the bridge, he knows where the bodies will be and sails up and down the river until he finds them and pulls them out. What a job.

We went to a Burns Supper on the 25th January. It was held at the church nearby. We were each handed a huge plate of haggis, neeps and tatties. As I'm not keen on haggis or turnips or potatoes without some accompaniment, it took me nearly all night to clear my plate. Couldn't believe the man across from me had three helpings of haggis! We were on the top table so I had to try and eat it. Before we ate, they read a Robert Burns poem and ended by stabbing the haggis. We then ate it and

Kevin preached. That was my first Burns Supper ever. It was a good evening. Lots of fun.

Dave Simpson is coming up next week for the weekend. Told him to take lots of vitamins before he comes after his episode with flu on his last visit! Will sign off now and do some ironing. Sorry for the delay in writing this but I'll be quicker next time.

Thanks again for writing.

Write soon. Missing you.

With love from,
Margaret

February 19th, 1991
(two weeks later…)

Dear Sally,

Glad to hear things are going well at Derby Church. We've just come back from two days on the Isle of Cumbrae, better known here as Milport. Just Monday and Tuesday as it's my half term break this week. We really enjoyed the time as church is very busy at present. You can imagine what an island two by four miles wide is like in February! Deserted! But it was great after Glasgow's hustle and bustle. The weather was really good so we were very blessed. We arrived home this afternoon.

Church is going well. On Sunday we had 89 in the morning, 105 in the evening and three saved. That was a very good week. We are doing a Personal Evangelism Course on a Tuesday and last week someone brought an unchurched person. He learned how to share about Jesus with his friends, listened to the talk, did the role playing, helped someone say the prayer – and then he got saved. Not quite the right way round but I don't suppose it matters really. I doubt at the pearly gates anyone will ask him the order it happened!

Anyway it's our AGM on Saturday so we might be leaving after that! We'll know what the complaints are then! Derby Youth Club seems to be going well from what I hear? Are you involved? We're starting a youth work a week on Friday. We're training the youth team at the moment.

It's been good how God has been providing in different ways. We had a £350 bill for our drains in Jasmine and the next day I got £365 back tax from my job. Kev said it was God. Next, my salary from work had not arrived on the correct date and Kev was not due to be paid for two days. I actually prayed and when I got to church after the service Kev gave me £10 which a tramp from the hostel insisted he had and was most abusive when he tried to give it back to him. We'll make sure he gets it back somehow in the next few weeks but we had to laugh. It really did help that day. God uses the most surprising people! Remember that occasion we had our car radio stolen? Well, by the following Thursday we had two car radios to replace it. (Have you had one stolen by any chance? If so, we have a spare one!) Lastly, when we came back from our time at Cumbrae, we had a cheque for £65 through the post. Apparently they'd not paid me enough before Christmas for some work I'd done. That nicely paid for the break away. God is so good.

We have a man in our church called Mr McCann. He loves Kevin but he hates drama and "items" in church (unless it's a solo by a middle aged, long skirted lady). Every time we have it in the church, he catches Kevin at the end of the service and goes on and on about the drama. "You don't need gimmicks," he was telling Kevin in a very loud voice at the door after the last drama special. He hates Catholics and thinks that Charles and Diana's marriage problems were caused by a papal plot! We have suspiciously begun receiving an anti Catholic magazine every month since he's been coming to the church although he denies all knowledge of it! Anyway, regarding the drama, we've said we'll write to him and let him know next time we're planning drama in our service. He seems happy with that. I thought the idea was to write to people to come to the church, not write to them to stay away! Different anyway.

Good visit from Dave Simpson. No flu this time. I think he's getting to like this place! It's great to hear you might have a woman pastor joining the team. I enjoyed reading the reports from your AGM. The crèche one was definitely the best!

See you soon,

Lots of love,
Margaret xxx

PS Did you really write to me during the sermon? You'll never make a deaconess!

March 19th 1991
(one month later…)

Dear Sally,

Thanks for your letter. Hope everyone is well. No doubt you are as busy as ever. Are you looking forward to Conference? We are. How are the kids? I imagine they will have grown a lot when we see them.

Our youth work began two weeks ago quite promisingly with 40 the first week and 32 the second (we wrote to everyone we could think of… teens, twenties, kids, cats, dogs…). Last night we had our Newcomer's Night. Fifty new people have arrived since August and so last night we had a party to welcome them all to the church and help them get to know each other. Kev talked about the church and we had a meal with them. Over the last few weeks we have also started a Nurture Group for new believers at the same time as the sermon in the evening service. The new Christians come to the worship and nip out for a coffee and a chat during the sermon, (and for some "fresh air" too as one calls it). Still trying to conquer that one, a lot of them. I must admit you do have to fight your way through a fog of smoke to get into the church some weeks! Need to relocate the NCSC (New Christian Smoking Corner) to somewhere other than the main door!

The morning service is growing nicely – there were 88 last week though the evening is very changeable with 95 last week but 115 the week before. We're hoping that now the youth team are trained and the Personal Evangelism course is over that April will not be quite so busy.

I think we have a rough picture of the church now. There are so many different people… the inner healing set, the name it and claim it department, the demon wing, pastor supporters, pastor stretchers, the previous pastor lovers (not literally) and now a whole host of new people too. We have done much preaching about respecting the right of other people to be different and with having lots of new faces too with no history, we can maybe see things being really blessed. Before we left Derby, someone who's been a pastor for years told us that there are only about ten different types of people. It's just that they have different names!

There was a stabbing at a pub not too far from the church at the weekend. The guy was killed. It was a green painted pub. Some of the pubs are blue and some are green. People have told us not to go in certain green ones (not that we are regulars at Glasgow pubs really anyway). The blue ones are Protestant and the green ones Catholic. Someone said, being English, we might not come out of certain green ones again! Didn't actually want to test their theory so we'll just take that as read! There's been a lot of demolition a little way from the church and they've knocked down all the tenements but they've left all the pubs that were on the street corners, so it looks quite strange with a lot of waste land and odd pubs still standing dotted over it here and there. Some of the guys who go to these places are wasted by ten in the morning.

Lastly, you asked where we think of as home. I still feel Derby's home because lots of our friends are there but Glasgow has our possessions and all the new friends, so that's home too. Glasgow is a great city though and there is an ownership and a pride in being part of it, with those who live here. It's a lovely church and the Glaswegians are great people. I love their honesty, their sincerity, their sense of humour and their willingness to open their arms and love you. We've just acquired an architect recently. We are obviously going up in the world!

Well, really must go. I had about twenty letters to answer and I'm working through them but that's enough for tonight. No more this week. Looking forward to Conference which is coming up soon. Love seeing everyone each year. Be a long journey home this year!

Write soon. We miss you both very much.

Take care,
Margaret

PS We survived the AGM. Should be banned! Actually, not too bad at all really. Just not very good for the Pastor's blood pressure! Went very well. There's hope for our future yet!

*

It takes all sorts to make a world

*

God's Thoughts

> *"So since we find ourselves fashioned into all these excellently formed and marvellously functioning parts in Christ's body, let's just go ahead and be what we were made to be, without enviously or pridefully comparing ourselves with each other, or trying to be something we aren't."*
>
> Romans 12:5-6a

> *"The command we have from Christ is blunt; Loving God includes loving people. You've got to love both."*
>
> 1 John 4:21

Your Thoughts

I was quickly learning that everyone's not like me. Even though the bible tells us to love our neighbour as ourselves, often it's difficult to understand people with whom we have little in common and sometimes, it's even harder to love them. We all have them from time to time, at work, at church, in our street, at home! It can be difficult to acknowledge that just because someone's thinking or acting in a way that's not our way, they may not be wrong, they may just be different. It takes all sorts to make a world.

Mentally make a list of likeable people in your life:

Mentally make a list of those you find it difficult to like:

Think about this second list and ask God to help you to understand their story. Imagine their hopes, fears, disappointments, desires, their past, their future…

Prayer

Now ask God to help you accept their differences.

Make a choice to acknowledge they may not always be wrong, they might just be different and even if they are wrong, pray for grace to walk in mercy, not stand in judgement.

Pray for that person. By an act of your will, ask God to bless them.

Bible Meditation

Now get comfortable, find a quiet place, and spend time meditating on the Bible verses earlier in this chapter.

6

April 16th, 1991
(five weeks later...)

Dear Sally,

Hope you have fully recovered from Conference. I think we're still catching up on sleep from our night of travelling. We left the South Coast at 1am and arrived about 10am. We had two very quick stops at 4 and 7am. Considering how long it was, it wasn't too bad, but once a year is enough.

When we got back, we went into the house and my first thought was that I hadn't left the bedroom very tidy. There were things on the bed from out of the dressing table. It was then I saw the window had been forced and someone had been in the house. What actually happened was that our neighbour upstairs arrived back home about one minute after our burglar entered at around 3.15 in the morning. (Where do you go at 3.15? Maybe ran short of Abba CDs!) So consequently, the latter didn't visit us for too long. That was an act of God if ever there was one. Glad our angels were on guard that night (or was it Benny and Bjorn?) Anyway, now forgiven all Abba parties, at least until next time!

Still, everything's back to normal now and our burglar didn't get chance to steal anything, thank you Lord. We were obviously a bit upset after the burglary. It's horrible thinking that someone's been in your home, so we went down to Queen's Park Café on Victoria Road for some ice cream (the best ice cream in Glasgow) and then onto Queen's Park for a wander round. Dog delighted…ice cream and walkies. He has put in a request for a burglary once a week! We saw Mark McManus from *Taggart* walking his dog down Victoria Road. He drinks at the pub there, which is predictably called the "Queen's Park". The actual park is at the end of the road. There's what's called a "high spot" there where you can see all over the city, it's a great view. It's the place that a lot of churches do intercession from. It's also the spot that a lot of covens do stuff from too, I hear. The park is very popular with the south side's gay community and anyone who doesn't like them too, hence a lot of attacks and even some murders happen there from time to time. Never feels very safe to me.

We are starting our extra early morning May prayer meetings soon. It really makes a tremendous difference. We have early morning and other extra prayer during the months of January, May and September and it works really well. The folk really rise to the occasion for the month. It seems much better than prayer things that go on and on and dwindle down to a handful of people. We work on "Input" and "Momentum" and try and input in prayer before the momentum in the church has stopped and we really do see a difference when we have a month of "invading the invisible". Wee Eddie's our best attendee!

We have now 136 regulars attending the main services, though there's always thirty or forty not around for one reason or another. Hopefully the Billy Graham Crusade will bring a few more people in too.

My cousin Janet came up to stay for a few days recently. I had to pick up Mrs Christie before church as a one off on the Sunday morning and we used Janet's car. On the way back to the church there's a road marking which isn't very clear and Janet was just about to drive straight across a main road at the crossroads. I yelled to stop and she managed to screech to a halt – half way across the main road! All was fine but I think Mrs C thought she was heading for glory, caused not by an accident but by a heart attack! So did I.

Did the children enjoy their holiday? They seemed to. I enjoyed my ride on the dodgems, quite an experience!

Well, I'm going to sign off now as it's getting late. Michael and I are sharing a box of chocolates in bed at the moment and he seems to be getting more than me so I have to give that some attention. I am teaching only until 11am tomorrow, but then have a student teacher to see till 12.30 and a parents afternoon till 6pm so I should get home about 7 tomorrow evening. Luckily we've nothing on tomorrow night (speaking calendar-wise, of course). It was great to see you both last week at Conference. We really loved the time we spent with you.

Much love to Ron.

Write soon,
Love Margaret

May 23rd, 1991
(five weeks later…)

Dear Sally,

Thanks for your letter and the little card. It was lovely. Nearly everyone I know is waiting for me to write to them so I thought I'd really better make some time and do it. This is my last letter for tonight as it's 11.25pm and this morning was our early morning prayer meeting. It was the last one of the month, then we've just got a half night of prayer next week.

A week last Sunday Kev baptised eight new people. We crammed 175 into the building. They were sitting on top of each other – some almost in the tank. Last week 131 turned up and we were very pleased that some had come back from the week before. Usually it's around a hundred (plus all the angels of course!).

We had to smile. Kev's sermon title on Sunday was The Value of Virginity and Mrs Christie came to him straight after the message. He thought maybe he'd gone one step too far when she asked to speak to him. He sat down with her, bracing himself for a telling off and listened with amazement and amusement as she thanked him profusely (remember she's in her eighties and has been widowed for many years and was listening to a sermon about the value of virginity) and said, "Thank you so much Pastor for that wonderful sermon… I really needed to hear that this morning!" I mean….what an encouragement!

Billy Graham has arrived in Scotland. We go to the first meeting in Edinburgh this Saturday. Glasgow meetings start on June 4th. We have a coach going every night and we've been round the neighbourhood drumming up support. One person's coming anyway. Lots of prayer going up for that. Kev is an "Echelon Supervisor" at this Crusade. I'm not sure what it is but I know he has to guard Billy Graham. Apparently the police guard him from bombs and Kev guards him from everything else (I think?) If it's on TV don't forget to look for him.

Are you organised for Fraisthorpe? We've booked two weeks on the Isle of Skye for our summer holiday. Accommodation seems quite cheap up there. It'll certainly be different from

Glasgow.

Took Michael up to Cathkin Braes yesterday. I opened the door and he leapt out of the car and was totally uncontrollable for the whole time. He was just running about wild and it took us ages to get him under control. Someone said the witches had probably been sacrificing stuff up there recently and he could smell that. Anyway, it's the lead next time! The walk consisted of Michael racing round with Kevin in hot pursuit (well I helped a teeny bit!).

Our youth work is going quite well. We are getting a regular thirty. Last week they brought their friends for the first week and one got saved so we were quite pleased. The youth team need more training but at least it's started.

Kev and I were coming out of church the other Monday morning and there were two gangs, one on each side of the bridge on the main road near the church. They were throwing home made Molotov Cocktails at each other. We shut ourselves in and stayed there till they'd finished! Someone was saying last week that the gang stuff is getting a bit lively at the moment. In Pollok the building workers are threatening to boycott the upgrading work on the houses as they keep getting attacked by street gangs of young teens. A lot of the gang warfare is between themselves and is over territory disputes. There are teenage gangs for whom fighting is an end in itself and then there are the more sophisticated gangs who war to control the drugs, money lending and extortion and things like that. Apparently these people have replaced chains and hammers for golf clubs in the boot of the cars. Looks better when the police do spot checks I suppose! I was wondering why there are some really great cars parked in some really rough areas. Gangs are going up in the world! There was a police chase up the M74 this week. It was a gang thing too. Amazing that there's stuff going on all around under your nose and you don't even notice. A bit like the God stuff really – in reverse – so much going on, on another level… and also on the negative side too. We do not fight against flesh and blood but against powers and principalities. When you remember that fact, there's so much that becomes clear. It's just that I keep on forgetting! Amazing what's all around that we never see isn't it?

Well better go now. It's 11.45pm. Tell Chloe I think of her every time I use my pencil sharpener at school (which is every morning).

Love to Ron. See you soon,
Love from,
Margaret

June 7th, 1991
(two weeks later…)

Dear Sally,

Thanks very much for your letter. Glad to hear that you are all well. The house you have picked sounds as though it will be great once you've done your bits and bobs on it. It's funny, you've swopped areas with your mum!

We put in an offer last week for a flat round the corner. This was an "offers over" sale which means that everyone who is interested puts in an offer and one of them (usually the highest but occasionally the one who can move in first) is chosen by the vendor. No one knows what anyone else has bid except that it has to be over the asking price so not having worked this system before, we weren't sure what to offer. Anyway, we won by £25! At that point it is legally binding so you have to be sure that you want it. If you're not careful, you could end up with two houses…or three…or four! We're still waiting for our house to sell in Derby. This flat's great to live in short term, but it will be nice not to have to pay the rent anymore. There's a lot to do inside as the couple are in their eighties but we can take our time. It overlooks a golf course and King's Park so Michael will love it. Hope the neighbours are OK. Will miss the Abba songs running through my head in a Sunday morning service!

The Billy Graham Crusade is going well. We have taken a double-decker bus every night and the folk have been packing it with their friends and relatives. They've prayed so hard for them – we both feel quite tense every night during the appeal just praying they won't be disappointed. So far we've had a member's best friend converted – also an old lady's friend, someone's son, someone's girlfriend, someone's workmate, a newish convert's dad, someone's mum and someone's boyfriend – plus six homeless women from the hostel. Sorry I don't know their names but hopefully in the future they'll be deacons, leaders and committed members of our church and I will know their names. We'll have to see if they turn up Sunday. We've got a special night with a supper to follow so we're hoping so. The bus driver came last night and he's coming again tomorrow night. The meetings have been good – the atmosphere is brilliant and it has been very exciting to see the stadium packed out every night. About two and a half thousand per night have responded to the message. I doubt we will get any referrals – just people our folk bring. In Scotland the attitude to Pentecostal churches appears to us to be that of Derby twenty five years ago. We have been told that the organisers are a bit reticent to refer converts to Pentecostal churches.

(a week later…)

It is now Monday and nearly a week's gone by. Very busy week so I'm just finishing your letter. The crusade is over...12,000 saved in Glasgow and many recommitments. As we thought, we didn't get many referrals but in addition to that, some who already came to our church on a regular basis and got saved at Billy Graham got referred somewhere else! Never mind. They were still with us on Sunday. God must have evened it out because at our evening service special on Sunday, ten people got saved. Kev was like a Cheshire cat all evening. A little dint in the kingdom of darkness I hope, and a mighty big dint by Billy Graham this month. What a man!

It's been really hot up here this week. I've noticed when it gets hot in Glasgow, everyone falls out! Yesterday the drivers in the first two cars at the traffic lights in front of us both jumped out and started fighting each other because one had cut in front of the other. I've seen them shout but I've never see them actually fight before! We have named it "Summer Sickness".

Are you still at Sainsbury's? I would imagine you're extremely busy just now with church, a house to run, a maths course, three kids and three jobs!

Well I had better go now as it's 11.15pm and after such a busy week I was like a zombie at 7am this morning. Off to the Isle of Skye next month. Will let you know how we get on. Thanks for your letter again.

Lots of love,
Margaret

PS When do you move?

*

It's important to think on another level

*

God's Thoughts

> *"This is no afternoon athletic contest that we'll walk away from and forget about in a couple of hours. This is for keeps, a life-or-death fight to the finish against the Devil and all his angels."*
>
> Ephesians 6:12

> *"For everything, absolutely everything, above and below, visible and invisible, rank after rank of angels – everything got started in him and finds its purpose in him."*
>
> Colossians 1:16

Your Thoughts

It was a major key when I began to try to see more in the invisible realm. We do not fight against flesh and blood and although sometimes our prayers may seem to bounce off the walls, what we bind on earth will be bound in the heavenlies. We not only have physical eyes and ears, we have eyes of the heart and ears of the heart too and we can see and hear so much more if we would only ask God to show us, and listen to Him. It would change so much!

Why not, for the next month begin each day by binding the enemy and loosing the Holy Spirit into your day? It will change your day!

Day

1 2 3 4 5 6 7 8 9 10 11 12 13 14 15 16 17
18 19 20 21 22 23 24 25 26 27 28 29 30 31

Prayer

Ask God to help you to see beyond this visible world and to open your eyes in a greater way to His invisible world.

Pray everyday, accordingly.

Bible Meditation

Now get comfortable, find a quiet place, and spend time meditating on the Bible verses earlier in this chapter.

7

July 17th, 1991
(six weeks later…)

Dear Sally,

Hope you got my postcard.

We had a great time on the Isle of Skye. It was a very beautiful journey, travelling up by the side of Loch Lomond and then onto Glen Coe and Fort William. The weather was fine, the sky was so blue and Loch Lomond was breathtaking. When we got towards Glen Coe the mountains seemed to take on a menacing atmosphere. Glen Coe has huge rocky hills on both sides of the road and it has an incredibly still, sad feeling. Huge boulders lie on the lower slopes either side of the road. You can imagine the MacDonalds and the Campbells running down the hillside. I think the Campbells murdered the MacDonalds in their beds didn't they, or was it the other way round?

We caught the boat to Skye after lunch. We stayed one week in a caravan and one week in a cottage. The caravan was miles from anywhere right on the side of the seashore and the atmosphere was just so still and serene. The birds must have been used to visitors because they came into the doorway of the caravan for crumbs every mealtime. Michael had a great time too and spent most of his time sleeping in the meadow of wild flowers somewhere by the caravan. On the Sunday, we visited a church on the island. It was absolutely silent when we walked in and when Kevin put his keys down, it seemed like the whole church turned and stared at us disapprovingly. There were no musical instruments but a "presenter" who hummed the first note of a Psalm and then everyone joined in. There were no hymns at all. At the end of the service, there was a closing prayer and then after the "Amen", everyone turned and faced the central aisle and row by row, filed out of the church. The key holder ended the procession and locked the door as he left and no one spoke a word the whole time. The funny thing was, outside there was a sign which said, "The church with the friendly welcome"!

On the way back home from Skye it was pouring with rain and as we travelled through the Highlands, the little streams which were gently winding down the mountains during the journey up, had become huge waterfalls every quarter of a mile or so at either side of the road. Later on we passed the Highland Games at Luss and saw them tossing the caber (big pole!).

Anyway, we were soon back to earth. On the first day back in church, a girl came in to let Kevin know that she was Carl Denver's daughter and had the cure for Aids and if Kev would pay £50, she would tell him what it was. (Kevin says Carl Denver was a Scots singer in the 60s. I didn't know, did you?).

We have a couple at church who were saved at the Billy Graham meetings and they have been living together for the last few years and came to see us this week to say that they've decided to put it off no longer and to get married. They have moved into separate rooms apparently since they got saved.

It was the July 12th Orange Walk this week too. A lot of the roads were closed off and there was a band of flutes and drums marching through the streets. Apparently, the idea is that if you can burst the skin of the drum outside a pineapple (Glasgow slang for a chapel), then you're in for a reward. Not sure what it is or whether that's true or not! The march always comes towards the end of Fair Fortnight which is the first two weeks in July.

Sat next to Wee Eddie on Sunday at church. Still can't understand a word he says. Didn't even recognize "daffodil" this time! It's great how people look after him and watch out for him. I was thinking on Sunday there's nowhere but a church where he could find a family of his own, somewhere to belong. Churches aren't perfect but good ones are very special places.

It's Kev's birthday too this week. Thirty seven years old! He's getting on! He's making a birthday resolution (it's a bit late for a New Year one) to *do* things, instead of just thinking about them. One minute you're in your twenties and the next, you're heading for forty! That's what he says anyway. I'm only half way there yet at 34!

Must go anyway and write some more letters.

Love to everyone,
Margaret

August 19th, 1991
(a month later…)

Dear Sally,

Thank you for the postcard from Fraisthorpe. Hope you all had a good time and that the weather was kind to you. If it's anything like the Scottish camp no doubt you'll all be ready for a rest now.

Dear Sally

The year seems to have gone very quickly. It's "back to school" on Friday. It doesn't seem long since we broke up at the end of June. I've decided to stay on a little bit longer at my current school. The travelling is going OK and it's a nice school so we'll see what happens. Hope Chloe and Jake are enjoying school and looking forward to going back in September. It still seems like the middle of summer to me! I'm working afternoons this year which is actually OK with all the evenings I have out at church.

Yesterday was Sunday and we had a good day with 120 in the evening plus 22 kids at the kids' club. We've started a group for the kids called the 7 O'Clock Club. They stay in church for the praise and leave for their own thing before the sermon. It's been going two or three months and it seems to be fetching more families out plus un-churched too as they're bringing their friends. We're having a drama special monthly now so writing a lot to Mr McCann recently. He's almost becoming a penfriend! Seems to be working quite well actually.

Last week was our first week with 100 in the morning and Kev was over the moon being a real sacramentalist as he is. The communion service has always been special to him. Summer seems to come to an end and church gets going again around the middle of August up here rather than September as with you. I'm still picking Mrs McNaught up every Sunday morning. Have nearly heard the whole of Robbie Burns works now (well it feels like it)!

Hope you passed your maths exam and have something lined up for next year. I'd like to study computers as we're hoping to move into that area a bit – but I don't know the top from the bottom of one at the moment.

There was another gangland killing this weekend in Provanmill. It was Arthur Thompson's son, better known as Fat Boy. Arthur

Thompson is known as The Godfather and is a big name in the gangland scene in Glasgow. Fat Boy had just been released from Barlinnie Prison and, according to the press, had been boasting about who he was going to put an end to, when he got out of Bar L. Looks like they got to him first. It was on the street near to the "Ponderosa" house just before midnight. There was also a stabbing outside an East End pub at the weekend. The guy was a soldier and had survived the Gulf War. He died outside the pub.

Michael the dog is doing well (as well as dogs do). Think he might be going deaf as he ignores me completely when I shout "stay" if we are on the park. Kevin says he has selective hearing syndrome as he has no problem at all hearing a packet of sweets being opened from the other end of the street. Very good newspaper carrier though…sometimes. Also very good at washing dishes…with his tongue!

Well I'd better go now as it's very late. Hope your house sorts itself out soon. Any progress?

Love Margaret

PS Just received Chloe's letter. Many thanks. Will reply in due course!

PPS Forgot to say, we are moving house soon. I think I told you that we have bought a cottage flat round the corner and up the hill. We've kept saying since we arrived that we may as well buy somewhere and be paying a mortgage instead of rent. Well now we've done it! Bit of a leap of faith with not having sold Jasmine. We're praying that the people renting there will stay this time, otherwise with two houses to pay for, we're "scunnered" as they would say round here. On the other hand, if we don't move, we could be enjoying early morning Abba parties in ten years time!

September 17th, 1991
(a month later…)

Dear Sally,

Hope everyone is well.

We are now well into the Autumn programme. House Groups, Nurture Group, youth and kids' stuff have all started up again and we seem to be working every hour God sends. Dave Simpson was up last week. I think the church have adopted him as their own now! Have started planning for our new flat. Really excited. Can't wait to move in. So glad we've actually made a decision to move.

Kev had to bar someone from the church this week. The girl had become more and more disruptive and ended up nearly beheading Kevin with the car park chain the other Thursday night. Kevin decided enough was enough, at least for a while anyway, before she started to do damage to people!

Mrs McNaught was reciting again this week on the journey to church. She doesn't mean to be, but she's so funny. Last week, in the middle of communion, the pianist began playing quietly in the background and she started shouting, "Shut up. Shut up, be quiet I tell you". She hates anything but silence for that part of the service. She was very comical though at the time.

Quite a few more killings actually since I last wrote (in the city, not in the church… although there's one or two). On the morning of Fat Boy's funeral, two bodies were left in a car which was placed on the route where the funeral procession would pass by. It was in Shettleston. That's where I travel through every day by train on the way to work. Apparent revenge attack but who knows? The two were thought to have taken part in the killing of Fat Boy. No one in the East End was willing to give any information to the police at all. Either they are too scared or those that are "in the know" just deal with things themselves. Even members of the bereaved families were warning other family members not to cooperate with the police.

On a lighter note (well maybe not) got talking to the lady next door yesterday. She's just lost her husband. There was one time that he waved to me through the window. I was going to call in when I heard he wasn't so well. I kept meaning to do it and putting it off as I'd always got more important things on. When she said that it really made his day when I waved, I wished so much I'd called. Hope to chat to her more.

Not long now till our move! Just counting the days now till we're round the corner and up the road! Can't tell you much about the flat just now as I've only been in once but can give you all the details once we're in. We've got our moving date now and it works out that Kev's away for three days when we move so Lynne's coming up from Derby to help. Should be fun anyway. So excited!

Anyway that's all for now I think.

Hope you are all well and that work is going OK.

Better sign off.

Much love,
Margaret

*

Doing it is doing it

*

God's Thoughts

> *"When you tell God you'll do something, do it – now. God takes no pleasure in foolish gabble. Vow it, then do it."*
>
> Ecclesiastes 5:4

> *"Each day is God's gift. It's all you get in exchange for the hard work of staying alive. Make the most of each one! Whatever turns up, grab it and do it. And heartily! This is your last and only chance at it."*
>
> Ecclesiastes 9:9b -10a

Your Thoughts

It's so easy in the business of life, to fail to recognise the "urgent" from the "important". We fill our lives with things which seem urgent and never get to do what is truly important. Sometimes it's just a case of planning. So why not take time just now to reassess and mark out those things which are really important.

Write down three things that you have been meaning or wanting to do for a long time.

1.

2.

3.

Consider – doing it isn't reading about it, writing about it, talking, thinking or planning it. Doing it is doing it.

Now write down when you are going to do these things. And do them.

Prayer

Seek God's forgiveness for not prioritizing and ask Him to give you wisdom in discerning the important from the urgent.

Ask Him to help you with your planning, short term and long term.

Pray for the ability to use the time He gives you every day with His wisdom.

Bible Meditation

Now get comfortable, find a quiet place, and spend time meditating on the Bible verses earlier in this chapter.

Note: Read The Neighbour's Story in "The Seagull"

8

October 20th, 1991
(a month later…)

Dear Sally,

Glad you are getting settled into your new house – it'll be great when it's finished. You can sell it, then go on a world cruise with the profits!

Well here I am in our new home. Lynne arrived from Derby last Thursday afternoon and we spent the evening packing up the last few things. The removal van arrived on Friday morning and we just stayed back to clean round and say goodbye to our flat for our first fifteen months in Glasgow. It has been a good home for us through that time. Will miss the new kitchen, the fresh light décor of the house and the chippy across the road. I won't miss the Abba parties though! New things to come I'm sure.

We piled the pets in the car plus some last minute things and we drove round the corner and up the hill to Croftside Avenue. When we got there I walked up the stairs (this one is an upstairs flat) and stood in the living room and I felt that I'd lived there for years. The previous owners had been there for forty years and it does need a lot of attention but it's got a great atmosphere and I loved it from the moment I walked in. Kevin rung in the afternoon (he was away for three days) to see how things had gone and Lynne and I unpacked a few things until bedtime then went to sleep surrounded by boxes and bags. Michael has settled in well and will love the golf course at the back of the house to run on. His basket is nicely positioned by the window though he refuses to get in it for some reason at the moment. Mr and Mrs Solomon, the previous owners, are 80 and 89 years old respectively and are Jewish. On the door frame of the front door and the main room, under the paintwork there's a little box with some bible verses. I love it!

Bri and Nev from the church are arriving tomorrow to put some more tiles on the roof and rough cast the chimney (if that means anything to you). Someone else connected the washing machine yesterday. The deacons gave us £300 for the house last Saturday which was very kind and we bought an electric fire, some stand up heaters and an electric blanket.

Church is going well and seems to get more and more busy as each week passes, with paperwork and different things that crop up. Kev often works a long day though I must admit if possible, we always take Monday as a day off.

How is Chloe going on at school…she'll be in top infants now won't she? My teaching in school still takes a lot of my day even though I'm working afternoons now. I'm hoping it'll settle soon as I have a constant backlog of church work to do. I'm travelling and working eleven till five and then working and preparing for another hour or maybe longer so working two hours takes up a major part of the day by the time I've got ready to go to work. I think I'll have to look for something nearer at the end of the school year.

The evenings are drawing in now. Can never work out how, in

the summer, it's light here much longer than Derby, say from about 4am until 11pm, but in winter, it's light much less than Derby. When December comes, it's dark for 4pm and daylight comes again by 8.30am in the morning or so. Should have listened more in science lessons!

Well better go now. It's 1.20 am.

Take care,
Love Margaret

October 31st, 1991
(eleven days later…)

Hi,

Just a short note to let you know we have bad news about Michael.

Two days ago, we found a swelling on his abdomen and took him to the vet the next day (which was yesterday). Kevin took him in and I waited in the car. When Kev came out, he didn't have the dog. The vet said he would do an exploratory operation today to find out the problem, so they kept him in.

I have been in school all day today and I was waiting all morning for Kev to ring, willing the minutes to pass. He rang at lunchtime. The vet apparently rang through to Kev in the middle of the operation to say that there was a mass in his stomach and that he wasn't going to get better. He gave us a choice to wake him up for a couple of weeks or put him to sleep there and then, so Kev went for the latter rather than have him go through two weeks of pain for our sake. He was bounding round the park two days ago so it was a bit of a shock.

We are so sad. He was our first dog and was a wonderful companion especially over the last year. I can't believe I will never see him again. He has caught many of my tears over the past little while I can tell you and we'll both miss him so much. Ten years is a long time.

Can't write more just now because the paper's getting wet!

Will be in touch,

Take care. xx

November 16th, 1991
(two weeks later…)

Dear Sally,

Hope you are well. I think you know most of our news through the phone call but nevertheless, here I am!

Our house, is coming along nicely. The back window overlooks a golf course, then a big park and beyond that across the city of Glasgow to the Campsie fells and the Kilpatrick hills. You can see Ben Lomond too on a clear day. It's a fantastic view. There was snow on the mountains yesterday – bad sign! At night, thousands of lights come on all over the city and it's a stunning sight, right from our sitting room! Bonfire night was fun as we had a great view of all the fireworks without leaving the fireside.

We're at least dry and warm now which is a start but we need the electrics checking fairly soon. We should definitely have had the door bell mended first. I was fetching in the washing last week while Kev was on the phone and I shut the door by mistake. As we are upstairs I just couldn't make Kev hear. Luckily after fifteen minutes, one of the cell leaders called and although they couldn't get in either, eventually they went back home and phoned him from their house to ask him to let me in. Even then, they were on the phone for what seemed like ages and I got in eventually after about an hour and he'd not even missed me! At the other extreme, we went out last Monday for the day and left the front door wide open for the whole day! Don't know how we did that but I'm sure it was Kev's fault! Strange that he thought the opposite. Anyway, it was so obviously open that everyone who passed must've thought we were at home. In line with Ecclesiastes, must learn there is a time for it to be open and a time for it to be closed. We just get it the wrong way round.

The house has been so empty without Michael. The day he was put down, we had to take the prayer meeting in the evening which was a bit of a challenge. We didn't tell anyone that night about what had happened as I couldn't talk about it. The next few days, every time we came in the front door, we just expected him to be there, wagging his tail as he always did and excitedly examining the bags to see what we'd brought him home. It was so sad coming into the house each time. Then Kevin suggested we just go and look at the dogs in the dogs' home, not to buy, just to look! Which leads to my best news of all…

On Tuesday, we went to the Cat and Dog home in Carnwadrick, just to look of course and.............. we came home with a little puppy!

We've called her Mary. We wanted a boy dog just like Michael but she was so gorgeous that we ended up choosing Mary. She is so sweet but I must admit I still have a little cry about Michael every day. We took her in the car for some Kentucky Fried Chicken the first evening (she's supposed to be on baby food and scrambled egg!) then she came up to the bedroom when we went to bed. We weren't going to repeat Michael's first night in Derby. We left Michael shut in the kitchen and he made so much noise that we still ended with him in the bedroom by 4am. I remember Kev went downstairs with bare feet in the morning and stood in a pile of something not very nice! So we decided to tackle it differently this time. We took her upstairs and, of course, she went to sleep immediately. I have a feeling we may be doing that for the next 12 years! I watched Mary falling asleep before I put out the light. Puppies are so gorgeous. She could hardly keep her little eyes open. I felt so happy when I thought of the years ahead of her. Besotted!

What are you studying this year? Are you still thinking of teaching? Dave Simpson is coming up to stay at the end of next week. Will be good to see him.

Better go now. Mary needs a wee. Will send you a photo soon.

Love,
Margaret

December 1st, 1991
(two weeks later…)

Dear Sally,

Thanks for your letter. Hope you are well.

What is the weather like down there? We have wind, rain and the occasional snow on the mountains. Can't wait for spring. Our electric blanket, fire and heaters are getting plenty of use at present.

Dave leaves for home tomorrow morning after his holiday of nearly a week. Actually we have really enjoyed having him though I don't know about him. The church are starting to ask him if he's staying now, they've seen him so often! I suspect romance could be in the air!

How is your house coming along? No doubt you are getting sorted out now. We need our electrics upgraded fairly soon. This month we've had the garden tended – our twelve foot hedge, twenty yards long is now down to six foot and hopefully the grass should be in shape pretty soon instead of knee high! The garden slopes down and edges onto the golf course so once it's done, it should be quite nice if Kev will stop laughing at the golfing efforts.

Hope Chloe and Jake are enjoying school and Brittany is OK. I'm still working afternoons – still travelling too much. It's pay day this week thank goodness. Not long until Christmas, I think we have about three weeks left, maybe four.

Church is going well. We had 132 yesterday morning and 175 in the evening – that was a particularly good Sunday for us though. There are lots of new faces at the moment and it's very hard to get to know them – we have to think of a better way to initially connect with the newcomers to the church. We had another newcomers night tonight with fifty newcomers invited to get to know each other. We played a couple of "get to know you" games and then had a three course meal together. We had a parallel party for their kids and ended with little talks from the deacons and Kev about our church. It was great fun and as all had arrived in the last six months, none of them knew a lot of people so they all had a good chat and laugh. New people bring life and having so many people come to the church over the last eighteen months has been wonderful. It seems a really happy church just now. It's like a new day has come and it's a privilege to be part of it.

Mary is wonderful! She is everything a little puppy should be. Lots of cleaning up puddles just now and quick exits for the door. I'm getting an old hand at pulling socks out of her back end! She's already established herself as leader of the household. She thinks Kev and I are in her pack! She has one or two little surprises in store I think. She spent her first couple of weeks tasting everything in the house. How do you stop a dog doing that? Can't spray the whole house with puppy repellent!

It looks like everything is gearing up for Christmas round here, especially the money lenders. Steve, who lives in Castlemilk, was telling us of the people who go door to door with a pile of £20 notes, offering to lend the money. Very tempting if you've got no money to buy the kids' presents. The trouble is, the rates to pay back are huge and when you can't pay, things get worse!

I am really looking forward to our Glasgow Christmas, followed by our Derby one again. We are staying at Steven Kemp's flat over Christmas and we are bringing the puppy down too so that should be fun! She is soooo sweet and she's house trained already. Not bad for saying we live in a flat.

Have you seen Kev's mum lately? I try to write every Monday but since August I don't seem to do anything but school and church work.

Well better go now. It's 1am so it's bedtime. See you at Christmas.

Love to everyone,
Love from, Margaret

*

Dying is a part of living.
Only then can come new life...

*

God's Thoughts

> *"Listen carefully: Unless a grain of wheat is buried in the ground, dead to the world, it is never any more than a grain of wheat. But if it is buried, it sprouts and reproduces itself many times over."*
>
> John 12:24

> *"There's an opportune time to do things, a right time for everything on earth. A right time to hold on and another to let go."*
>
> Ecclesiastes 3:1,6b

Your Thoughts

I don't know about you – I find it so hard to let go. Even when I know it's God, saying goodbye is so difficult. Ecclesiastes 3 talks about the seasons of life. A time to be born, to die, to cry, to laugh, to keep, to throw away and many more occasions of life. Maybe take time now to read that for yourself. We read it and we accept it but it doesn't make it any easier to do it.

Dying is a part of living. What things have come to an end in your life? How did you feel?

Ended	Feeling
1.	
2.	
3.	

Prayer

Acknowledge before God those things in your life that have come to an end, whether you planned that, or not.

Ask Him to speak to you and show you if there's anything which you failed to let go of.

Acknowledge what He shows you and place these things into His hands once and for all. He will take care of them. Now turn, and walk on into the future He has planned for you.

Bible Meditation

Now get comfortable, find a quiet place, and spend time meditating on the Bible verses earlier in this chapter.

9

In 1992

*	*The Queen started paying income tax*

*	*The IRA exploded two bombs in Manchester*

*	*Britain was signed up to the European Union*

*	*The Premier League was launched in football*

*	*The Big Breakfast made its debut on TV*

March 7th 1992
(three month later…)

Dear Sally,

Hope you are well. Haven't written for a while so I thought I would catch up. Thanks for your letter. How is your studying coming along? No doubt you're looking forward to starting teacher training in September? I really enjoyed being at college – I'd quite enjoy going through it again.

Church is buzzing at the moment. Last Tuesday we held the first part of our Personal Evangelism Course with 43 of the new Christians who had been evangelised by last year's course. It was brilliant to see, knowing not one of them had been here this time last year. A few weeks ago on a Sunday morning Kev gave an appeal before the sermon and five people made a commitment to Jesus. I think it's the presence of God they feel in the meetings. It's great to see what God is doing.

Mrs McNaught gave her testimony. She was really good and made us smile too. She was explaining that George Jeffreys was speaking the night she got saved. "Now…" she said, earnestly glancing at Kevin who was standing by her side. "Our pastor does his best…but George, well he *was* a man of God!"

We've joined all the senior citizens into a prayer team and we get them to pray about anything relevant. It's great to see God working through their prayers and even better that they know they are an important part of the church. Just trying to include as much prayer as possible into the fellowship in one way or another. A while back, we closed all the meetings for a week but they met as usual and prayed instead. We've also had a whole night of prayer recently. Six at night till six in the morning.

Today is Sunday and the day is over. Tonight four people made a commitment to God. Kev was pleased because his sermon was actually directed towards Christians and it was God's presence in the meeting that really challenged them. There's so much happening through the prayers of the people.

Hope you have settled into your new house now. What is your next room of conquest? Your lounge looks great, just like a magazine. Ours hasn't changed much. We still haven't decided whether to decorate, re-wire or replace the windows.

The puppy is growing quickly. She has had her two sets of injections now. She was fine going to the vets the first time but the second time, I think she remembered the place as she trembled from head to foot and looked really sorry for herself even before anything happened. For the rest of the day, you would have been forgiven for thinking that she'd had a heart transplant instead of an injection! Seems to have recovered from her trauma now though. She's at present asleep in a plant pot (a large one). She ate the plant last week. She'll have to stay there as she's been such a nuisance tonight that I'm loathe to wake her up to go for a late walk but no doubt, anytime now she will spring into action.

We've started obedience classes and she weed on the floor two weeks out of three. We never took Michael when he was small and so we said this time we are going to have a trained dog. Ha ha. Last week, I walked her for ages before the class and then half way through the lesson, I could see her suddenly start to squat down for a you-know-what's-coming as she stood in the middle of the room surrounded by all the other dogs. Having stood in the freezing cold all winter, willing her to take up this position ASAP to get us out of the cold, I quickly recognized the danger signals! I flew across the room, grabbed her, shoved her tail between her legs and ran with her out onto the grass. By the time I got her out she, and I, as you might imagine were in an interesting state and by the time I'd cleaned us both up, using only grass (as my car keys were in my pocket in the hall), the class was nearly over! Made a mental note never to go there again! She is incredibly chewy and very poo-ey at the present time but she is still the most loved dog in the world.

Hope all is well with you.

Much love,

Margaret

June 28th, 1992
(three months later…)

Dear Sally,

Hope everyone is well. Time is going so quickly. Another three months since I wrote but today we broke up from school for seven weeks. Hence my letter writing starts again. Decided to type this one. Please excuse the typing.

Hope church and everything is going well. I'm not sure whether I'm coming down to see my Aunt in the summer. I might visit when Kev goes to the Scottish camp. He is speaking there again this year. We are going to the Isle of Lewis in a few weeks. Lewis is in the Outer Hebrides, off the West Coast of Scotland somewhere beyond Skye. That will be new territory for us so really looking forward to it.

That's almost another church year over. We've been here nearly two years now. What an amazing two years. It's been the most stretching time you can imagine in every way. I feel like a different person from when I came.

Wee Eddie died last week. They traced who he was by the betting slip in his pocket! Don't ask me how. A lot of people from the church were at the funeral. It was very moving to see how many people turned up. Even though he had no-one, he really did have a family at his church.

Kev is saying that somehow we need to get more space in the church and we need to maybe think of extending the building. He's been chatting to the architect in our church recently. Scary stuff, scary money – especially when many in the church are on a low income. What do we know about heading up a building project? Kev worked with submarines and I work with children! Oh well, let's not think about that yet.

The trial has just ended of Paul Ferris who was accused of the murder of Arthur Thomson Junior last year (remember Fat Boy?) amongst a lot of other things. It was the longest running murder trial in Scottish criminal history and has lasted 54 days. He was acquitted on every charge. He had an excellent lawyer though. Donald Finlay is a very well known lawyer in Glasgow often very successfully defending those in the underworld. Some really interesting stories have hit the papers over the last couple of months. And some funny ones! Last night, the newspaper stated, "One of the witnesses, when asked to clarify his initial comment, that a fellow low lifer was not a very nice person explained 'I meant he's a ******* toerag!'" (but it wasn't bleep). Someone else on the stand in court, when describing another witness, stated that the judge should take no notice of her as she wasn't compos mental! Will miss the newspaper reports and the six o'clock news stories!

Mary is eight months old now. You know I said she was housetrained, well I was lying!

Better go now anyway,

Much love,
Margaret

September 4th, 1992
(three months later…)

Dear Sally,

I hope you are well and that you had a great holiday at Fraisthorpe. We have now recovered from our holiday and it seems like we've never been away. I can't believe it's September. The year just goes so quickly.

Kev is at a board meeting tonight. He had fifteen things on the agenda plus any other business so I think it'll be a long one.

Extension rumours still looming. Paying for the thing fills me with horror, let alone filling it with people but I suppose that's when you learn the lessons about trusting God. It's not faith until it's faith is it? And that's what changes you.

We've had the Kensington Temple Black Gospel Choir at church since we've been back from holiday. It was a great evening to kick start the new church year. Including the children, we had 430 people on 270 seats. Some people were standing outside with their heads through the open windows and there were thirty in the corridor and some chairs outside on the grass by the fire exit. Usually we only get about 130 plus kids so it was a big squash. The extension is calling! We are still having new people come and are having a Newcomers Night soon for fifty more new people.

John Mitchell is coming to do his mission from college for three weeks. We've never had an Assistant Pastor before so that will be new. Hope all goes well. Dave is coming to visit again in October.

We have now decorated and moved into the main bedroom. We've also done the spare room, bathroom and main room so we've still got three to go.

We had a great holiday on the Isle of Lewis. We travelled up via Inverness and drove past Loch Ness. It was lovely down by the water until a million plus midges arrived and queued up for their midday meal! (Not a lot of queuing was seen actually). No sign of the Loch Ness monster that day though we did look quite hard. We had this great idea that as the ferry sailed early the next day, we would travel up to Ullapool the day before, enjoy the journey and then find a quiet spot and sleep in the car. Great in theory and planning! Forgot about the nine month old dog-in-body-but-puppy-in-head who was accompanying us on the adventure. Every single noise or person who walked past the car was welcomed with a shower of high pitched barks, woofs and other noises, all night long. And I mean all night. We saw midnight and every hour through the night until we got on the boat in the morning. The dog nearly didn't come. We were very tempted to send her in search of the Loch Ness monster about 4am. Kev also wanted to tie her up by the pier about 5.30am and go back to collect her in the morning but I couldn't let him do that. Don't want her needing to go for counselling when she's older!

It was a great break except that it rained every day, nearly all day for the whole two weeks. One day, it rained so much that the rain flooded everywhere including all the rabbit burrows and nearby our house, some newly born rabbits got washed away. There was one left. It was tiny and it was sitting on the grass in the howling wind and rain. We brought it into the house. (I couldn't leave it outside in the pouring rain). I wanted to take it to the vets but Kev suggested that with an estimated five million rabbits (estimation!) on the Isle of Lewis at any one time, the vet might not be so pleased to see us. We gave it carrot juice to drink and milk. We (well I) named it Rumbo and made it a little nest. The next day Rumbo was still with us and walking about his homemade cage, looking quite interested in things and the next day too he seemed to be getting stronger but on Thursday morning Kev picked him up and Rumbo wet himself and stopped breathing! As artificial respiration didn't seem an option, he had to stay dead. It was really sad. Actually, Kev was more concerned about getting wet but I was sad. We put him in a Tupperware box with some nuts and buried him in the garden near to the burrow he had been born in just a few days before (OK I admit, that was the royal "we").

Anyway it's September now and we have replaced rabbits for

humans once again and are looking forward to the brand new church year. As with rabbits, we lose them occasionally and recently, we've lost one to Wales, one to Perth, five to England and one or two to other parts of Scotland. It must be the time of the year. John arrives at Glasgow Elim for his Bible College Mission in a couple of weeks or so. Will be great to have him with us and we are really looking forward to working with him again. Will be just like Derby Youth again! Will let you know how things go and whether he's married by the time he leaves! You never know. It could be in Glasgow that he meets "the one"!

Well Kev has just arrived home so I'll sign off and find out how soon we are going to be £200,000 in debt!

Take care,
Love Margaret

*

If you want to be something you've never been before,

you need to do something you've never done before

*

God's Thoughts

> *"I'm not saying that I have this all together, that I have it made. But I am well on my way, reaching out for Christ, who has so wondrously reached out for me. Friends, don't get me wrong: By no means do I count myself an expert in all of this, but I've got my eye on the goal, where God is beckoning us onward – to Jesus. I'm off and running, and I'm not turning back."*
>
> Philippians 3:12-13

> *"Careful planning puts you ahead in the long run."*
>
> Proverbs 21:5a

Your Thoughts

Looking back, faith seems so easy and we very quickly forget that in the "becoming whatever we are or are not" today, we've had to use faith to step out into new territory again and again as we embark on things that we've never done before.

It all goes back to the whole "stretching" thing really. As we step out into new places, new resources within ourselves emerge or old ones become stronger and God adds to these His strength and power and we become more of the person God created us to be.

What totally new experiences did you have in the last year?

What?	**When?**
1.	
2.	
3.	

Is there anything which you felt was too great a challenge to undertake? (If so, remember next time, He has everything you need and He will never call you without giving you the equipment to do the task).

What totally new experiences could you plan or embrace for the next year?

1.

2.

3.

Prayer

Ask God to keep you constantly open to new experiences.

Make a decision before Him to walk through the new doors He opens for you, hand in hand with Him.

Ask Him to guide you and to lead you in a completely new way from this day on.

Bible Meditation

Now get comfortable, find a quiet place, and spend time meditating on the Bible verses earlier in this chapter.

10

September 30th, 1992
(a month later…)

Dear Sally,

Hope you are well and that things are going well at Derby. Have you settled in at college? I remember it was quite strange at first but I became used to the new routine. I am writing this letter on the station waiting for my train on my way to school so please excuse the writing. We have just had a Wednesday mid morning prayer meeting and I've just left that to go to school.

John was up to his neck in teas and coffees and washing up and women when I left. He has settled in well, is very busy and already has a fan club! He is working about seventy hours a week so he'll be ready for a rest when he finishes. Good job his mission is only three weeks long. He led the meeting Sunday morning and the people really like him. The female attendance is definitely on the up and up at the moment!

On Saturday, we had our first women's breakfast. At the breakfast we had a meeting until 11am and the ministry ended at 2pm! I closed the meeting officially at noon so they could wander off when they wanted but I was three hours helping pray at the front! The speaker must've been tired by the end of the day. I had been dreading it for weeks and weeks. All the time on holiday, I kept counting the days. All I had to do was lead the thing. Now I've done it, I don't know what I was so scared of but I've never done anything like that before and it was just the "being in total charge and what if anything happened" kind of thing. (Not sure what could happen?) But anyway, I managed it!

Last Friday, we had a half night of prayer 10.30 till 2.30am then a meal – chilli and stuff. We got to bed at 4am. I picked Mrs Christie up at 10pm from her house. It made me smile when I thought how most people of her age are tucked up in bed by that time and she was just off out for the night! She certainly kept up the pace and was more awake than me when I dropped her back home at 3.15 in the morning. She's 86! No idea what the neighbours thought!

David Simpson rang us tonight, he said he told you about his penfriend. Trouble is, he's not written back yet. Can you give him a word from God?

(two weeks later)

I've still not finished this letter and it's two weeks later now. Back at home, no longer on station…

Hope church is still going well. John has now completed his three week mission in Glasgow. He went down very well and I think he learned quite a lot. (Not sure whether it was what he should have learned or not but we all enjoyed it). We've had some more new people and both services were packed on Sunday. We've moved in twenty more chairs today so there's room for one or two more to come now. Four people were saved on Sunday so we were smiling again!

The drugs scene is quite bad just now. At the weekend, two of the girls in the hostel overdosed and died, then on Monday yet another one of the girls died in her sleep. Yesterday, another one overdosed while injecting herself, also from the hostel, which means there has been four die in a week from across the road.

Tonight, during our prayer meeting, a man called Bobby who wanders in now and again came and injected in the men's toilet. I knew he'd been there a while so one of the deacons kicked the door in and found him spaced out with a needle still hanging from his groin. He actually looked dead but he was just high. We called an ambulance anyway but they wouldn't take him as he wasn't keen to go with them. The hostel worker from across the road had put his needle in their safe box and once he'd come round, he wanted to know where his needle was. When he found it was in their box he insisted in putting his hand in and getting it out. The police said there's raw heroin on the streets just now and that's why there's so many deaths. It's happening all over the city.

We would appreciate the prayers of your house group for our proposed building extension. We now have building permission and need around £153,000 to pay for an extension. The people are still coming in but we don't have anywhere now to put them so we are about to embark on some money raising. There's not much money around here so we're praying a lot. Bit scary. Sounds very simple in books when somebody else is doing it but doing it yourself is a different matter! What if we build it and the people stop coming? Kev knows that God has spoken to him. "If we build it, He will come," he keeps saying to me. Those are the words he has in his heart so that's good enough for me. We went to the architect's house for tea last night and worked out some details. The building begins, all being well, in April and our special offering will be on March 7th, just before it starts. Please tell anyone in Derby who is rich! If you know of any useful addresses who might help it would be appreciated. We do need more space to grow much further. God has really blessed us this year. There are about 200 different people in the day on a Sunday with usually 40-50 not around. We have 215 seats crammed into a space designed for 160 and it's like a sauna bath with clothes on, on a Sunday night. Good though!

How are the children doing? Tell Chloe we're still looking for a flat for her for when she's grown(!)

Well I'll sign off now and get ready for tomorrow before bedtime. Hope your course is going well.

Write soon.

With love and best wishes,
Margaret

PS Just heard another girl overdosed and died across the way.

In 1993

* *Britain's longest recession since the 1930s was officially over*
* *Buckingham Palace opened to the public*
* *An oil tanker ran aground in Shetland causing a major ecological catastrophe*
* *The X Files began on UK TV*
* *Jurassic Park was a major hit in the cinema*

Feb 6th, 1993
(four months later…)

Dear Sally,

Hope you are all well. Just to drop you a line to keep in touch. How is the weather there? It's like the Arctic up here. Hope Chloe, Jake and Brittany are well back into school and that you are enjoying your studies. Tonight has been a very rare night at home for us both. Church is extremely busy at the moment with loads of things going on.

Recently we've had an elderly man saved of 74. He's called Bert. Last week we went to see him. He lives on the same street as the church. He was wrapped in a blanket to keep warm as he was worried about the cost of the heating. We went in his kitchen and the lino had more holes in it than it had lino so when he came to church, we put some money in an envelope and I gave it to him as he left. Five minutes later he was back again, in his old clothes and slippers, full of "thank you's". It was worth double the money to see his appreciation.

On Monday, we had a party night for all the newcomers to the church which was good fun. Every Tuesday we are holding evangelism training ready for the *Jesus In Me* campaign in March. It's a selection of workshops each week on things like sketch board work, holding a coffee morning, schools work, drama, leading someone to God etc. It's ninety per cent practical with just ten minutes talk in each seminar. I went to the drama last week and it was really good. We've not done any "missions" in the church up to now, just personal evangelism really, but this is an Elim national initiative so we're part of that. On Saturday we have a day arranged for all the churches in Scotland with training. The organisers are travelling up from London for the weekend to take the day and the main speaker is staying with us on the Saturday night and speaking at church on the Sunday. It will be good to have him as we know him quite well.

Mary ate the sofa last week. We had left her with Ally for a couple of days in our house. We have, or should I say had, a sofa made of foam. She managed to tear the cover and then pull out the foam piece by piece until the room was covered in it and there was very little sofa left! She must have spent all day on the project! Ally nearly had a fit when she got home and saw no sofa, just a room covered in bits of foam. Good job it was only a cheap one, but poor Ally didn't know that. Dog-wise, we are still having a battle every time we go for a walk. I can't remember Michael being this hard to train! She thinks, as the lead is attached to her, then the responsibility for the direction, the length and the speed of the walk all lie in her hands (or paws). Lots of learning still to do yet.

Operation Blade begins this month. (In the city, not in the church!) The slogan is "Bin the knife, Save a life". It will be a one month long amnesty for handing in dangerous weapons. In the first four days about twelve hundred people have been stopped and 42 arrested. I read that last night. Apparently between 1991 and 1992, there was a noticeable rise in the number of murders in the city and the amount of armed robberies rose even more so this is the latest initiative in Glasgow. There is also Operation Eagle running alongside at the same time which is an anti-drug campaign. Need an anti-drink one too. Kevin asked a few weeks ago everyone to stand who either had a close relative who was (or had been) an alcoholic or who in the past had had problems themselves. I tell you, many, many people were standing.

Our extension begins in April. Not long to go now. Still collecting the pennies for the special offering next month. People have the most innovative ways of raising money. We've told them they can do anything as long as it's legal! Drug selling, mugging, dog fights, lead off church roofs and selling your body are suggestions we've outlawed! But other than that, you name it, they're doing it. Every one is so excited. Still scary when you're out at the front though. But we're heading for the goal now and going anyway.

Are the children still as busy as ever? Many thanks for the lovely photographs. We do enjoy keeping up with their latest school photos. Well that's about all the news for now. It's about time for Kev to pick me up for the station so I'd better sign off now and get my bags ready.

Take care and write soon,

With love and best wishes,
From Margaret xx

June 6th 1993
(four months later…)

Dear Sally,

Hope you are all well. Many thanks for your letter. Sorry it's taken me a while to reply.

At the moment, we have a heat wave and I am sitting at the bottom of the garden looking out over the city. I can't see the mountains at all today. It's very misty as well as very hot.

Tomorrow is the start of the prayer week. Every evening 7.45pm till 9.45pm there is a prayer meeting. On the Tuesday, the cell groups are doing a prayer walk and on Thursday the people are walking round Govanhill and praying. Wednesday is a fast and the other two are prayer concerts. Kev's a bit mindful that not many will turn up but I think it'll be OK. We'll see.

Dear Sally

This week is called "Spiritual Warfare in Action" so hopefully the Sunday messages will motivate a few to come.

Our special offering in March raised £35,000. That is a lot of money for our people to raise. It was a great morning. Everyone took their gifts to the front and we sang a praise song. The atmosphere was very high. It was also very moving.

The extension has begun! The builders started building in April and the building's at roof height now. No roof yet, just the walls. I couldn't believe the mess when I called in on Wednesday. At the moment the sky is visible from the inside of the church, half of the roof has been removed and the whole floor is covered with a huge tarpaulin which is covered in water. It looks more like a swimming pool at the moment.

It's rained quite a lot over the last few days so I hope either they can put a plastic sheet on the roof or that it doesn't rain on Sunday. We're having a baptism so it looks like everyone might be baptised. Kevin has just met the architect down there for an update of the progress and he says it's all going according to plan although to our eye it looks like a bomb has just fallen through the roof and there's been a flood as well. Really good to be able to stay in the building throughout for our Sundays though it does have its challenges! We have replaced bibles, notebooks and pens for thick coats, wellies and torches! We have just one light which we can put on and no heating for tomorrow so it's fur coats and umbrellas. It will be different anyway! We thought we might lose a few but they're actually bringing their friends "for the experience!" I wrote to a Trust the other week and they sent us £1,500. I thought that wasn't bad for the price of a stamp. The deacons said they'd put me on commission if I got results like that. I was really pleased when the cheque came.

There's a turf war going on just now apparently. It's in the newspapers quite a bit, tit for tat killings and all that. Arthur

Thompson, the Glasgow Godfather died a couple of months ago. Not on the street but in his bed in Ponderosa. The funeral was like a Mafia send off, thousands of flowers, men in suits lining the streets, some well known Glasgow names, and no doubt lots of plain clothes police mingling with the crowds. There was a bomb scare and police blocked off the cemetery which was very near to Ponderosa. It was amazing that the man died of natural causes considering all the assassination attempts he survived! Anyway it seems there's now a vying for top places once again in the underworld.

Better sign off now.

Hope all is going well at church.

See you soon,

Love and best wishes from,
Margaret

*

Feel the fear

And do it anyway

*

God's Thoughts

"Don't fret or worry. Instead of worrying, pray. Let petitions and praises shape your worries into prayers, letting God know your concerns. Before you know it, a sense of God's wholeness, everything coming together for good, will come and settle you down. It's wonderful what happens when Christ displaces worry at the centre of your life."

Philippians 4:6

"Look, God, your God, has placed this land as a gift before you. Go ahead and take it now. God, the God-of-Your-Fathers, promised it to you. Don't be afraid. Don't lose heart."

Deuteronomy 1:21

Your Thoughts

It's really easy to read and it's easy to say but to feel fear and to still go ahead and do what you're afraid of, is not easy. And yet we're told around 366 times in God's Word, in one way or another, not to be afraid, so He knows from time to time – we're going to feel it. And when we feel it, it's probably better to admit it rather than push the fear down. When we lay it out before God, then He can bring His Holy Spirit down upon it, touch it and change it. When we bottle it up and add guilt on top, we end up no better than when we began.

Name the last four things that have *really* stretched you or made you fearful:

1.

2.

3.

4.

Name four things you didn't do because you felt fear stood in the way:

1.

2.

3.

4.

If you are fearful, doing nothing is not an option.

* Acknowledge it…
  (how you feel)

* Rehearse it…
  (in your mind)

* Do it…
  (knowing that you can do all things
  through Christ who strengthens you)

Prayer

Now bring your future before God and pray through the words above.

Make a choice before God to use these key things every time you meet a situation and fear stands in the way.

Bible Meditation

Now get comfortable, find a quiet place, and spend time meditating on the Bible verses earlier in this chapter

Note: For more of Bert's story see "The White Elephant."

11

July 29th, 1993
(seven weeks later…)

Dear Sally,

I thought I would just drop you a line to say sorry I missed you the other day when I called round. Didn't get your message until we were back in Glasgow. Aunt Jan forgot to tell me that you'd rang at all. My stay wasn't really long enough. I could have done with a couple more days in Derby. I brought my Aunt Jan back with me for a few days on Wednesday. It gave her a change of scenery. It was good company for the journey too.

I'm sitting in the study by the window. It's very misty as I look across the city but there are still quite a lot of golfers out even at 9.15am. No mountains in view today.

Kev arrived back at 2am this morning from the Scottish Youth Camp with John (who came up to help) and then John and Aunt Jan left for Derby half an hour later. She rang this morning to say she was safely back.

Yesterday I took her to Loch Lomond with Joseph and in the afternoon he took us round the Briggait which is a gigantic market where anything can be purchased for just a few pence. It was a real experience and was a place I've never been before either. On Wednesday evening, we went a tour in the car round the city and on Thursday, we went round the shops for the day. It was like being on holiday myself.

John is going to be our new Assistant Pastor and will start on September 9th in the church. He arrives in Glasgow with all his worldly goods on the 6th. His mission up here last year was great and the people really connected with him well. They are all looking forward to his arrival now. Didn't think that within two years of being here, we'd be able to have a second pastor. God is so good.

I thought I'd clean round the house for the rest of the day. Annual event! Kev's gone to bed now for a couple of hours to recover from his overnight journey and Mary's gone with him. She didn't think much of getting up at 2am again after only going to bed at midnight. Nevertheless, had to do it! Always frightened of missing something! She keeps running round the house looking for Aunt Jan, running into the loo and looking under the bed. At one stage, she was convinced AJ was in the wardrobe. I think she suspects that I've hidden her somewhere.

The wall has come down at last! The church looks completely different inside. As you walk in, there is a big corridor ahead with some rooms at the back. The main sanctuary is enormous. It's twice the size but with no chairs in, it looks ten times the size. No doubt we'll soon get used to it. The builders were putting the ceiling tiles up when we arrived. They want to be finished by next Friday so they are working day and night at present to keep the handover date as arranged. This week, the glass will go in the windows, the flooring will be laid, the heating will be put in and the lighting. The suspended ceiling should be finished and the walls painted and the doors fitted after that. Next week, the carpet will be fitted. After that, we will make a platform and that should be that. When we eventually left, we came up the road saying, “It's soooo big!”

We were down at the church till midnight Saturday night talking to Alex, the architect. We were back at 6.30am Sunday morning with a group of people cleaning the church for the services. We had the morning service then went to a newcomer's three course lunch straight after.

Well better sign off now. Our official opening is November 13th so we are all looking forward to that. It will be good to have John up with us in a few weeks. Everyone is looking forward to having him come up.

Love and best wishes,
Margaret

Sept 22nd, 1993
(two months later…)

Dear Sally,

Doesn't time fly? Hope you are all well. Many thanks for my birthday card.

It is 10.30pm and we've just been down to Ayr for a walk along the beach with the dog. I think we ended up wetter than she did! Mary's golden rule is to be the first to get out of the car, first onto the beach, first into the sea. Then last out of the sea, last off the beach and definitely last into the car. (That's figuratively speaking of course, we don't actually go in the sea a lot in Scotland!) She was really wet so I put her in a dustbin bag and tied it round her neck to keep her warm! She didn't mind at all.

We are settling nicely into our new building now. We have spaced out all the cramped up chairs to give people a proper amount of room and we are now spread half way across our extension. The entire main sanctuary is double the size of the old one. The meetings have gone well and the group of people have not been too lost in the space as we feared they might. We had 170 plus 29 children for a baptism last Sunday which looked nice and full. When I said we needed an extension to Kevin he just gave me a withering look.

With the money we had already saved up, a couple of grants and several special offerings, by Christmas we should have a debt of just £40,000. At the start of the year, we needed £153,000 so we are delighted. God's provision to, and through His people has been amazing.

We called into the Youth Club on the way home. It is John's first youth night tonight. He arrived at the start of September and has not stopped since! The youth group had shrunk to fifteen people during the summer and he was going to re launch it for the autumn. He got 40 there tonight which he was delighted with. The first week has gone well and he seems to enjoy it.

We have just finished our Adult Retreat weekend. There were nearly sixty people there and it went very well. It was the first one we have done with adults so hopefully it will be the first of many. Dave Simpson was up for it too and seemed to have a good time. I never saw him to speak to all weekend. He spent his time surrounded by women! I went to take him home Sunday night and he was off to a party! John spent his time getting to know everyone (men as well) and I think it was quite useful for him to spend a weekend with them.

I have a pretty good class this year. They seem to be quite a nice little bunch. The girl I job share with is expecting a baby and the head has asked me to do her hours from January to June so I'll see how church transpires now we have an Assistant

Pastor. With the class I've got and extra help now at the church, it shouldn't be too difficult. My salary will double too which can't be a bad thing! How many teaching practices do you have this year? Do you enjoy being in the classroom or do you like the college part better?

John received his first death threat tonight by telephone. Kev was submitting a list of books he'd like to inherit when he goes! Still it's not very pleasant to get a call like that. It will be a good story for him to tell over Christmas in Derby anyway. We are coming down to Derby on Christmas afternoon and going back on New Year's Eve so we'll come round over the holidays.

Take care and see you soon,

Much love,
Margaret

In 1994

* *Sunday shopping began in England and Wales*
* *The National Lottery began*
* *The first bionic (battery operated) heart was implanted in a man in Cambridgeshire*
* *A ceasefire was announced by the IRA and the Loyalists in Northern Ireland*
* *Hugh Grant became a household name as he starred in "Four Weddings and a Funeral"*

May 24th 1994
(eight months later…)

Dear Sally,

Things are well here. It's such a long time since we wrote but it's been good to keep in touch by phone instead. The church is going well and John will soon be coming to the end of his first year at Glasgow. He's been very successful in the areas he's working in. His love life is not quite so successful just now, but that's another story.

We had the most amazing time a week ago when we had a visiting speaker. I've copied you a tape so you can hear it if you get time. He came to our Watchman Intercessors meeting on the Wednesday night which was absolutely awesome. There were just the thirty of them there in the building but it was like a conference night.

Bert, the elderly guy from down the street was there. His hand was healed from partial paralysis and he just couldn't believe it. There were a lot of real healings and the things that happened were amazing. It was awesome.

Right at the end of the meeting the speaker prayed for me in the prayer line at the front. The Holy Spirit was so powerful and I spent ages lying on the floor. I still felt the power of God when I got up. I thought I'd feel better if I went home as I felt really dizzy and weird all the time but when I got in the fresh air, it got worse! Kev was wining and dining people and I went home but I just couldn't stand up. I felt like that till I went to sleep and the next day I could still feel the presence of God so powerfully upon me. Not sure what happened but it was the most amazing experience of God.

The speaker talked about a time of refreshing coming to the Glasgow church. He said it's already on its way!

Anyway, better go now.

Much love,
Margaret

July 24th, 1994
(two months later…)

Dear Sally,

Hope you are well and are enjoying the summer holidays.

We have just come back from our holiday in the Shetland Isles. What a beautiful place.

Midweek in Shetland we wandered into a church and got chatting to the minister there who was called James and he invited us to go for lunch after the service on the Sunday. During the afternoon, he told us about what was happening in his home church down south. Some of the folk had been to a meeting in London and had spent hours lying on the floor after receiving ministry. There was laughing and shaking and lots of manifestations as well. The men went back to James' previous church and it began happening there too. Started in Toronto, Canada or something and thousands of people are starting to go over there to see what's going on. Have you heard anything?

Strange, when we got back, there was an article in a Christian magazine about an Elim Church down south. The same things are going on down there. The only problem is that their pastor is coming to speak at Glasgow Elim in September! Not sure whether just to cancel him but Kevin felt God specifically speak to him last January about inviting him up so we're still thinking it over…

Anyway, great time in Shetland but now safely back at home in

Glasgow. Lots to do in the coming months…

Been busy even since we came back. Not too much news.

One couple had a fight, girl broke husband's rib,

One girl disappeared for two days without trace,

One woman joined the Mormons,

Three people considered committing suicide,

Five people got saved,

The girl who attacked Kev with a chain before Christmas asked to come back to church,

One couple were told in the morning they were to be evicted at 10.30am the same day,

A seventy five-year-old was baptised plus two others,

One man sent to prison,

One suspected heart attack,

One convert on heroin was thrown out of drug rehab for being back on it,

One lady was slain in the spirit on her living room floor and healed of depression,

One new convert beaten up by her ex live-in lover,

One new convert attacked with a knife by another ex new convert,

Two old ladies have fallen over and …….

……..one pastor and wife are ready for another holiday!

*

God is no man's debtor

*

God's Thoughts

"Give away your life: you'll find life given back, but not merely given back – given back with bonus and blessing. Giving, not getting, is the way. Generosity begets generosity."

Luke 6:38

"If you listen obediently to the voice of God, your God and heartily obey all his commandments that I command you today, God, your God, will place you on high, high above all the nations of the world. All these blessings will come down on you and spread out beyond you because you have responded to the voice of God, your God:

God's blessing inside the city,
God's blessing in the country,
God's blessing on your children,
the crops of your land,
the young of your livestock,
the calves of your herds,
the lambs of your flocks.
God's blessing on your basket and bread bowl;
God's blessing in your coming in,
God's blessing in your going out.

God will defeat your enemies who attack you. They'll come at you on one road and run away on seven roads.
God will order a blessing on your barns and workplaces;
He'll bless you in the land that God, your God, is giving you.

God will form you as a people holy to him, just as he promised you, if you keep the commandments of God, your God, and live the way he has shown you."

Deuteronomy 28:1- 9

Your Thoughts

God is no man's debtor. We were on a journey with Him and He was adding to His church. He had blessed us with many people saved, many people added to the church and still growing, a building extension which doubled the size of the accommodation, finance to pay for it, additions to the staff of the church, a home we loved, and that was only the start. Little did we know that in just a few weeks time, we were about to be hit in a "life rocking" way by the Holy Spirit which would shake and move the church deeper like nothing else. In September 1994, God's Holy Spirit fell on our church in an amazingly, wonderful, powerful time of blessing, touching people in a way that they would never be the same. We no longer had a visitation, but a habitation and God increased His presence again and again and again.

In your life and in mine, God is no man's debtor. Whatever you give for Him, He will pour back to you again and again without measure.

Dare to read the verses above out loud. Declare them. Pray them. Meditate on them and read them for your friends, read them for your family and read them for yourself…and dare to believe them and make them your own.

For God is no man's debtor.

Epilogue

As I said at the beginning, it's twenty years since those first letters…

I taught at the same school (where I originally planned to be for just a couple of months) until it recently finally closed its doors.

Glasgow Church continues, through those who have ministered there since, to thrive and flourish with currently over 400 attending.

Many of those early new converts are deacons or leaders or workers in the church. Many others have flown the nest to other cities as pastors or other lands on mission and have churches and people of their own.

Sally is now a head teacher with her own school and still managing to juggle far more things than I! Their three children are now up and grown with lives of their own.

Mrs Christie and Mrs McNaught have moved to a much better place where no doubt the latter is now reciting Robbie Burns to the angels.

David found a Scottish lassie, moved up to Scotland and married her and John also found the love of his life at Glasgow.

He has two beautiful children and has gone on to lead a successful church of his own.

Our sweet little puppy grew into a beautiful 17 year old dog. Even her last winter, she was running round in the snow and loving life. But sadly, not too long ago, there came a day which was to be her last and she died in the springtime. I look down now at wee Jack Mac Peat, who graces our home with all the pleasures that only a new puppy can bring…

Kevin is doing what he loves best and pouring himself into the lives of pastors in different parts of the UK who are doing the same themselves with the people God has called them to. He is still, and will always be, the love of my life.

There's a dream to live, and a future to find, whoever and wherever you may be.

King David died, old and full of days. On that day when you go to meet your Father in Heaven, may you be "full of days".

I hope they will be days full of dreams lived, and a future fulfilled.

That is my prayer…

GO NOW, AND LIVE YOUR DREAM…

How Are You Doing?

These Things Will Keep You
Where You Are Right Now

Do I?

1. Allow events to dictate my feelings?

   ……………… (yes / sometimes / no)

2. Allow my feelings to dictate my thoughts?

   ………………..

3. Expect bad things and behave accordingly? Allow my behaviour to influence my experience?

   ………………..

4. Step back from anything stretching or uncomfortable or challenging?

   ………………..

5. See people as either good or bad, right or wrong? Relate only to those I like?

   ………………..

6. Fail to recognise the invisible world and to wage war accordingly?

   ………………..

7. Keep thinking, praying, planning and talking about what I want to do? Watch others do it, read about it… but don’t do it? Keep putting it off?

   ………………..

8. Refuse to let go of things I have loved and lost?

   ………………..

9. Refuse to do anything new or outside my comfort zone and stay with safe and familiar things?

   ………………….

10. Use fear as my boundary? Anytime I feel afraid, turn away, say no and go no farther?

    ………………….

11. Conserve what I have and be measured in my use of resources, physically, mentally, emotionally and spiritually?

    ………………….

These Things Will Help You To Live Your Dream

Do I?

1. Look for God's way to interpret uncomfortable events in my life?

   .... (yes / sometimes / no)

2. Choose to change my thoughts and allow my thoughts to change my feelings?

   ....

3. Expect good relationships, events and outcomes and behave accordingly?

   ....

4. Face challenges and stretching times with an awareness that these things are helping me grow?

   ....

5. Recognise that just because people are different or think differently from me, that it doesn't necessarily make them wrong, it just makes them different?

   ....

6. Stay aware that I am in a war? Use prayer as a weapon to fight problems here on earth, in the spirit?

   …………………

7. Think, pray and plan and then do it?

   ………………...

8. Let go and move on? Face change as a challenge and embrace new things as they come?

   …………………

9. Do things I have never done before and stay aware that they are helping me to grow and develop?

   ……………….

10. Use God's will and direction as my boundary and let His love spur me on to greater things? Let His perfect love cast out all fear?

    ……………….

11. Give my all for God in every way and expect Him to bless me? Know that God is no man's debtor?

    ……………….

What will you change and when?

Plan it, and do it.

It could change your life.

Notes

Notes

Notes

Previous books by Margaret Peat

The White Elephant contains eleven real life stories from daily life in Glasgow, which highlight various issues of the heart. The chapters deal with the subjects of forgiveness, forgiving yourself, repentance, shame, a heart of stone, inferiority, loss, fear, finding perspective in problems, the Father's love and being special to God.

The Seagull contains eleven more true stories which continue to highlight various issues of the heart. The chapters deal with the subjects of attitude, ungodly beliefs, making choices, the power of words, generational influences, putting God in a box, the place of mercy, soaking, sowing and reaping, performance orientation and breaking out of your comfort zone.

Both books have been highly commended by Christian leaders and those who have read them. If you would like to obtain a copy of either of these books or have more information concerning them, then please contact KMPeat@aol.com or www.elimscotland.org.uk/